D0648132

PRAYERS&
PROMISES
for Women

TONI SORTOR

BARBOUR
PUBLISHING

ISBN 1-58660-832-0 (Softcover)
ISBN 1-59310-029-9 (Hardback)

Cover image © PhotoDisc, Inc.

Scripture quotations are taken from the King James Version of the Bible.

Published by Barbour Publishing, Inc., P.O. Box 719, Uhrichsville, Ohio 44683, www.barbourbooks.com

Member of the
Evangelical Christian
Publishers Association

Printed in the United States of America.
5 4 3 2 1

PRAYERS&
PROMISES
for Women

Contents

PREFACE

Some days prayers roll off our tongues without effort. We have much to be thankful for—our families, our faith, God's provision, and all the promises we are heir to through Jesus, our Savior. Other days prayers are harder to come by. We may be facing a crisis, having problems with the children, or just be too exhausted to pray. A woman's day is long; her duties seem never ending. *Prayers & Promises for Women* is based on God's promises—and there are many of them. Some you already know, others might be new to you, while still others will seem to be pointed to your specific concerns.

This book is designed for women who are pressed for time. If you feel the need to pray about a specific concern, most likely you will find it in the alphabetical contents pages. You may want to expand these prayers or tailor them to your personal needs. They are meant to be used as prayer starters, somewhat like yeast. At the very least, they should give you some comfort and a quiet moment or two to catch your breath.

There are several sections in this book devoted to the stories of biblical women you may be familiar with. It's clear that women have always been important workers in the Church, and it seemed appropriate to feature them in a book designed for women. Other prayers are less gender-specific but approached through women's experiences and needs. We hope you find this book helpful in your prayer life.

HOUSEHOLD PEACEKEEPING

A soft answer turneth away wrath:
but grievous words stir up anger.

PROVERBS 15:1

Most often I am the one who plays the role of household peacekeeper, Lord. This is a double-edged duty. Not only must I pacify the children and my husband on their bad days, I must also see that I don't contribute to the mayhem through venting my own anger. When we're having a "she hit me first" day, Lord, help me hold my tongue until I can reply with a healing answer, not an angry one. When my husband comes home bristling because something went wrong at work, give me calming words, not words that will hurt or make him even more upset. And when I am angry myself, let me be an example of how to deal effectively with anger. Help me be the peacekeeper, never the one who stirs up more anger.

AVOIDING SIN

Be ye angry, and sin not:
let not the sun go down upon your wrath.

EPHESIANS 4:26

Father, You know all about anger, because You
have felt it Yourself. What You condemn is not
anger itself but the sins anger gives rise to. It's what
I do when I am angry that counts. Does my fury
make me say words that hurt and will be remembered for years? Is my tone of voice a weapon instead of a healing salve? Do I belittle those I love in
the heat of anger? Or do I remain as rational as
possible, perhaps retreating until I can discuss the
problem in a loving manner? The next time I am
angry, I pray You will guide me away from sin until
I can speak words of peace and comfort once again.
Help me be an example to my whole family.

OVER THE TOP

It is better to dwell in the wilderness,
than with a contentious
and an angry woman.

PROVERBS 21:19

Sometimes my anger is so overwhelming that I don't like myself, Father. I hear my voice go up an octave and know I am over the top. The children hear that voice and run for the hills, hoping I will calm down before they get hungry. My husband's face hardens into a mask that tells me he would rather be anyplace but here—even in a desert with no bottled water. I am emotionally alone, and I deserve to be. Lord, I need to ask for forgiveness from my family, to admit that my reaction was extreme, and ask to be let back into the family. Give me the resolve to make things better, to ignore my pride, and to do whatever is needed to make us a family again.

FORGIVENESS

*Be ye kind one to another,
tenderhearted, forgiving one another,
even as God for Christ's sake hath forgiven you.*

EPHESIANS 4:32

A mother always forgives, Lord, even when the offense seems unforgivable to others. Despite their anger and shame, I'm sure that even the mothers of hardened criminals find a way to forgive their children. We have no choice; we are, first and foremost, mothers. My children deserve my forgiveness, too. They are young, and their sins are small—if irritating—when compared to others' sins. When anyone in my family does wrong, admits the wrong, and repents of the wrong, show me how to follow Your example, Father, and forgive for the sake of Your Son, who came to forgive us all of our sins and make us acceptable in Your sight. May I never hesitate to forgive anyone when You have already forgiven me.

ELISABETH

But the angel said unto him,
Fear not, Zacharias: for thy prayer is heard;
and thy wife Elisabeth shall bear thee a son,
and thou shalt call his name John.

LUKE 1:13

Zacharias and Elisabeth had waited years for a child, and now they both were old, well past the age for bearing children, no matter how much they wanted one. Then Gabriel, Your messenger, appeared to Zacharias with the good news that the son Elisabeth would bear would prepare the way for the coming of Your Son. Father, sometimes it seems my deepest desires will never bear fruit, no matter how much I pray. I go on with my life, but there is an emptiness in my heart that only You can fill. I know not all prayers are answered, but many are, so I continue to petition You, for You are my hope.

GABRIEL AND MARY

And, behold, thy cousin Elisabeth,
she hath also conceived a son in her old age:
and this is the sixth month with her,
who was called barren.
For with God nothing shall be impossible.

LUKE 1:36–37

Gabriel told Mary that she would bear a child by the Holy Ghost—Jesus, the Savior the Jews had waited for. Then he gave her the news that her barren cousin Elisabeth was also pregnant, despite her age. Gabriel's using Elisabeth as an example of Your power must have eased Mary's mind, especially when he concluded, "For with God nothing shall be impossible." Quite often I pray for what I know is impossible, Lord. I know that in the best of all worlds, most of my prayers will not be realized. But some will, if they are in Your will for me. For You, nothing is impossible.

ELISABETH AND MARY

Blessed is she that believed:
for there shall be a performance of those things
which were told her from the Lord.

LUKE 1:45

Lord, Your promises never go unfulfilled, if we have faith. Elisabeth and her cousin Mary never doubted the words of Gabriel, Your messenger. A barren woman in her old age and a young virgin would both do the impossible because that was what You wanted of them, and they had faith that You can do anything. The births of John the Baptist and Jesus the Christ were out of the ordinary from the beginning; so were the women who gave them birth. Father, I don't know how You will use my life, but I have faith in Your promises and am always ready to do Your will, no matter how impossible it seems to me at the time.

THE NAMING

And his mother answered and said,
Not so; but he shall be called John.

LUKE 1:60

Lord, I remember how eager everyone was to know the names of our babies. Family and friends all had their own ideas, just as Elisabeth's did. They wanted her to name her baby after his father, who deserved to have his name carried on, but Elisabeth insisted the boy be named John—the name You had given him through Gabriel before he was even conceived. Zacharias backed up his wife and obeyed Your messenger: "His name is John." Sometimes I have to go against the wishes of others to do Your will, Father, and it's not always pleasant, but Your wishes come before all others, and I will do my best to honor Your name all my days.

JERUSALEM

*And thy renown went forth
among the heathen for thy beauty:
for it was perfect through my comeliness,
which I had put upon thee. . . .
But thou didst trust in thine own beauty.*

EZEKIEL 16:14–15

Your chosen city, Jerusalem, was beautiful because of Your beauty, Father—a city made perfect through You. Its fame spread throughout the world and, as people often do, its inhabitants began to take credit for the city's beauty themselves, forgetting that its true foundation rested on You and believing that its beauty somehow came through their efforts. I tend to do the same today, taking credit for what I did not create on my own. Please don't let me fall into the trap of false pride. Whatever small beauty I bring into this world is only a tiny reflection of Your beauty, Your creation, Your perfection.

21

THE PERSON WITHIN

*For man looketh on the outward appearance,
but the LORD looketh on the heart.*

1 SAMUEL 16:7

We are too conscious of outward beauty today, Lord. Our singers, our heroes, our role models—even our politicians—are expected to meet certain standards of beauty. Even worse, we instinctively trust the beautiful, never looking beyond their bodies, as though perfect hair indicates a perfect brain or a pure heart. When we stop to think about it, we know this is foolish, but we rarely do think about it. Make me more conscious of this error, Lord. Teach me to look through appearance when I choose my heroes or my husband. A perfect hairdo should not unduly influence me—it may be warming a very small brain. An expensive Italian suit may very well be covering a dark heart. Help me see beyond beauty—or the lack of it.

THE BEAUTY OF HOLINESS

*Give unto the LORD the glory due unto his name:
bring an offering, and come before him:
worship the LORD in the beauty of holiness.*

1 CHRONICLES 16:29

Holiness is true beauty, not what I wear or how my hair is done or how white my teeth shine. Indeed, holiness is Yours, never mine. I am fatally flawed, but I worship One who is perfect in all ways, One whose glory alone is worthy of praise and thanksgiving. There is no beauty compared to Yours, no faithfulness like Yours. The little glimpses of beauty that decorate my life are grains of silver sand at the edge of an incomprehensible ocean of beauty. I only see a grain or two in my lifetime, but it dazzles my eyes and makes me turn away blinking. I worship You in the beauty of Your holiness.

THE WORK OF OUR HANDS

And let the beauty of
the LORD our God be upon us:
and establish thou the work
of our hands upon us;
yea, the work of our hands establish thou it.

PSALM 90:17

What I do for a living can be either secular or sacred. The choice is mine. The kind of work I do is not important. I can do anything in a way that glorifies You, Father. A worker in the humblest of jobs is just as capable of demonstrating Your beauty as one in the most exalted of positions. The next time I am feeling unproductive or unappreciated, remind me that I am working for Your glory, not my own. A tiny bit of Your beauty is reflected in my work, whatever it might be. May those I work with always see You in my life and be brought closer to You through me.

MARY'S SONG OF PRAISE

My soul doth magnify the Lord,
and my spirit hath rejoiced in God my Saviour.
For he hath regarded the
low estate of his handmaiden:
for, behold, from henceforth
all generations shall call me blessed.

LUKE 1:46–48

Of all the women in the world—young or old, rich or poor, of high status or low—You chose a young girl from an unimportant, backwater province to bear Your Son, our Savior. Her response was, appropriately, a song of joy and praise, one of the most moving prayers in the Bible. Mary understood that You had given her a great honor that would be remembered forever, and she welcomed it—as well as the responsibility that came with it—with joy. You bless my life in many ways every day, Father. May I receive Your blessings with a song of thanksgiving on my lips.

GOD'S MERCY

For he that is mighty
hath done to me great things;
and holy is his name.
And his mercy is on them that
fear him from generation to generation.

LUKE 1:49–50

Mary realized that her honor was not of her own making but came as a gift from You, Father. All she had done was live in obedience to Your laws the best she could, as had her fathers and those before them since Abraham. You had promised to do mighty things for Your people. Sometimes they had obeyed You and flourished; other times they had followed idols and felt the pain of Your anger. However, Your mercy is always on them who follow You, and their blessings flow from Your constant love. Make me mindful of Your great gifts, Father, that my song may praise Your work in my life.

SCATTERING THE PROUD

He hath shewed strength with his arm;
he hath scattered the proud
in the imagination of their hearts.
He hath put down the mighty from their seats,
and exalted them of low degree.

LUKE 1:51–52

Mary knew that she was not important in the eyes of the world, not in the ways people usually reckon importance. Pride is of no value. It is a false feeling of righteousness that only lives "in the imagination of their hearts." In choosing Mary to bear Your Son, You ignored the proud and powerful, demonstrating Your love for the unimportant people of the world, those who follow Your ways in spite of the world. Mary claimed no part of Your glory. Help me understand that You value faithfulness and to trust in Your love above all else, claiming none of Your glory as a personal reward.

In Remembrance of His Mercy

He hath filled the hungry with good things;
and the rich he hath sent empty away.
He hath holpen his servant Israel,
in remembrance of his mercy;
as he spake to our fathers,
to Abraham, and to his seed for ever.

Luke 1:53–55

Not only did You bless Mary, Father, You also blessed Israel, sending Your Son to redeem this people You had always loved. Your constant mercy to them had been demonstrated from Abraham onward, even when they sinned against You and followed idols. Now Your promises to them would be fulfilled through Mary's delivery of the Savior. Not all would accept this precious sign of Your mercy, but the offer was made for all. I am not worthy of Your gifts of mercy and forgiveness, Father, but I accept them with the joy of Mary.

BEING THERE

Cast me not off in the time of old age;
forsake me not when my strength faileth.

PSALM 71:9

There comes a time in every woman's life when her parents—those strong, loving people who gave their all to raising their children—will begin to need help. When that time comes for me, Father, give me the wisdom to understand the problems they are having and the often simple ways I can be of service to them. Show me how to make time for them in my busy life now, to give them what they need and want the most—my love and attention, time with their grandchildren, and my promise that I will never forsake them. Above all, Father, help us find the suitable balance between independence and protection that will assure their safety and maintain the dignity they so deserve.

DIGNITY

Honour thy father and thy mother.

EXODUS 20:12

In time, I may have to begin to play a more active role in the lives of my aging parents, Lord. My mother may need help with the shopping; my father may need to be convinced he should not drive anymore. I may have to help balance their checkbook or help with their investments. This can be a difficult time for all of us, especially if they feel they are a burden. I ask Your help when this time comes. Remind me that their dignity must be preserved whenever I need to help them. Keep me tactful, allowing them as much self-control as possible within the bounds of safety and honoring their wishes above my own. They gave me so much; now it is my honor to give to them.

INCLUSIVENESS

*But if any widow have children or nephews,
let them learn first to shew piety at home,
and to requite their parents:
for that is good and acceptable before God.*

1 TIMOTHY 5:4

Daughters are usually the caregivers of the family when parents grow old, but everyone has a certain amount of responsibility. Don't let me try to carry the load by myself, Father. My brothers and sisters need to feel included, no matter how far away they live. Show us how each can contribute to our parents' care, whether through more frequent visits, phone calls, or financial help. Don't let me get so wrapped up in caring for my parents that I shut out other family members. Everyone is hurting now—even those who seem unconcerned—and I need to draw us all together so my parents' old age will be a time of good memories for everyone.

HELPING HANDS

If any man or woman that believeth have widows,
let them relieve them,
and let not the church be charged;
that it may relieve them that are widows indeed.

1 TIMOTHY 5:16

As my parents age and need more and more help from me, remind me that other help is available, Father. Part-time companions or nursing aids can ease my family's time burdens and make it possible for my parents to stay at home. Senior citizen centers can provide quality activities and care for the elderly. Meals-on-wheels or other similar programs can assure proper nutrition for those still living on their own. The costs are minimal and often absorbed by insurance. My family and I will provide all we can, but there is no shame in asking for help when it is needed. You have provided these helpers for us; let us use them wisely, Lord.

WITH THE SAME MEASURE

Give, and it shall be given unto you;
good measure, pressed down,
and shaken together, and running over,
shall men give into your bosom.
For with the same measure that ye mete
withal it shall be measured to you again.

LUKE 6:38

Lord, I am very careful when baking to see that my measuring is accurate. Dry ingredients need to be shaken and pressed down, especially brown sugar, or the results will not be as sweet as they should be. Teach me to be just as meticulous in my charity. The cup of flour I loan to my neighbor should be a full, generous cupful; the clothing I donate to charity should be clean and in good repair, not clothes that belong in the garbage. My acts of charity reflect on You, and I want to bring You honor at all times.

GIVING WITH JOY

*Every man according as he purposeth in his heart,
so let him give; not grudgingly, or of necessity:
for God loveth a cheerful giver.*

2 CORINTHIANS 9:7

Lord, sometimes I start out to give generously
but end up putting the large bill back in my wal-
let and finding a smaller one to put in the plate.
Other times I see my pew-mates giving more
than I have out, so I quickly exchange the bills
again because I feel pressured to be more generous. By the time the plate is out of sight, I don't
feel at all cheerful. I know that no one really cares
what I give. I am putting the pressure on myself
and can blame no one but myself. Don't let me
feel social pressure that's not even there, Father.
No matter how much or how little I can donate, I
should give joyously.

GIVING IN PRIVATE

Take heed that ye do not your alms before men,
to be seen of them:
otherwise ye have no reward of
your Father which is in heaven.

MATTHEW 6:1

Father, I would prefer to wait for Your reward in heaven but, being human, I am not always able to wait. Can I at least tell my husband? He won't tell anyone else, because my good deed was really insignificant. But the smile on his face is already my reward, isn't it? Doing Your work should not be like my old Girl Scout troop, where we had to find at least one good deed a day to report at every meeting. Help me overcome the urge to pat myself on the back in the sight of others and wait to hear You say, "Well done."

THE REWARD

Then shall thy light break forth as the morning,
and thine health shall spring forth speedily:
and thy righteousness shall go before thee;
the glory of the LORD shall be thy rereward.

ISAIAH 58:8

You promise me wonderful rewards when I am charitable, Lord. I will be "like a watered garden, and like a spring of water, whose waters fail not" (Isaiah 58:11). Good health will come to me, as well as good reputation, and I will live a life of righteousness. Remind me of this the next time I pass up a charity event for an evening in front of the television set or hang up the telephone without even listening to the caller. I cannot answer every request made of me, so I count on You to guide me as to where I should invest my efforts in such a way as to bring You glory.

GOD'S GIFT

For unto us a child is born.

ISAIAH 9:6

Father, how wondrous is the birth of any baby, whether it is mine or Yours. I spend hours watching this new being sleep. He was created by my husband and me yet is so different from us. I dream great dreams of this child's future. I know this baby—our baby—is truly special and pray he will be a blessing to the whole world. Mary did not know the whole story of her child's future (it might have broken her heart to know everything), but she knew He was a gift from You that would bless all Your creation. Be with us today in our joy and stay near as we strive to raise this baby in a way that will please You and allow him to accomplish whatever You have planned for him.

My Reward

Lo, children are an heritage of the LORD:
and the fruit of the womb is his reward.

PSALM 127:3

You equipped me for many things, Lord, one of which is the ability to bear children. You made my body strong. You gave me a husband who wants children as much as I do. You assured me we could be good parents with Your help. Because of Your blessings, this tiny baby has joined us and made us a family. I know there is much work ahead of us in raising this baby—physical work, emotional work, and spiritual work—but the rewards of parenthood are already far greater than its demands, even on the toughest of days. May Your presence in the midst of our family bless this child throughout the years to come. Thank You, Lord. We will not fail this child. We will treasure Your gift.

PRAISE THE LORD

He maketh the barren woman to keep house,
and to be a joyful mother of children.
Praise ye the LORD.

PSALM 113:9

Not all women will have children, Lord. Some never find the right man, the man they want to have children with. Some choose to be childless. They invest their efforts and time in other pursuits and are happy with their choice, a choice You have allowed them through Your gift of freedom. Others will have difficulty and years of sadness that may never lead to motherhood. Whether motherhood comes easily, is not chosen, or comes later than desired, help me remember that our lives are a deep concern to You. If it is in Your will, there will be children. If this is not the path You have chosen for a couple, You will make their lives meaningful in other ways. Praise ye the Lord.

MARVELOUS WORKS

I will praise thee;
for I am fearfully and wonderfully made:
marvellous are thy works;
and that my soul knoweth right well.

PSALM 139:14

My baby knows my face, and her crooked little smile is heaven to me. Some people in the family do not believe my baby smiles at me ("Gas," they proclaim), let alone that she knows my face and associates it with good things, but she is truly wonderfully made. While once she was a little creature looking for food or comfort, only concerned with her own needs, now she suddenly knows how to give me comfort. I don't know how this happens, Lord, but I thank You for all the detailed, complex, and mysterious work You have put into this little baby and Your decision to let me be the mother of such an amazing little being.

CORRECTING IN LOVE

Children, obey your parents in the Lord:
for this is right. Honour thy father and mother. . .
that it may be well with thee,
and thou mayest live long on the earth.

EPHESIANS 6:1–3

Even young children have responsibilities, but You carefully pair every command with a promise—a tactic that most mothers readily learn. This is not bribery but cause and effect; children who obey and honor their parents find family life far more enjoyable than those who don't. Then You add a second promise that can only come from You: "and thou mayest live long." Raising obedient, loving children requires me to show gentleness and patience, not threats or harshness. I pray that You will teach me how to soften each correction with the same love I receive from You, who guide and correct me. May Your patience and kindness be made visible through my actions.

FATHERS AND DISCIPLINE

Hear, ye children, the instruction of a father,
and attend to know understanding.
For I give you good doctrine,
forsake ye not my law.

PROVERBS 4:1–2

Most family discipline comes from me because I am home more than my husband, and correction is best done promptly. Many fathers avoid disciplining their children, not wanting to spoil the few hours a day they are with them, but children need to know that their fathers are concerned about them and love them enough to correct them. Lord, help me see when my husband needs help in this area. Don't allow me to shut him out of this responsibility just because that may be the easy path. Don't let me overburden him, either, always making him play the role of "bad parent." Teach us to work as a team in raising our children, sharing the good times and the bad.

Children

Riotous Children

Even a child is known by his doings,
whether his work be pure,
and whether it be right.

Proverbs 20:11

There are certain children that I do not want to let into my house, knowing something will be broken, the cat tormented, or some new transgression taught to my children. These are not really bad children, just poorly raised ones. No one has taught them the basic rules of acceptable behavior. Some of them I can work with gently—not taking the place of their parents but civilizing them a little through love. Others I will have to banish until they come to their senses or Your love reaches their little hearts. Father, I pray for these riotous children who need Your love and instruction so much. Show me how I can help them in some small way without taking over their parents' duties or heaping blame on anyone.

43

PRAYERS&PROMISES

YOUNG LAMBS

The young lions do lack, and suffer hunger:
but they that seek the LORD
shall not want any good thing.

PSALM 34:10

Some children are born lions; others are born lambs—but the meek shall inherit the earth. That is Your promise, even if I do not see it fulfilled in my time. It is a lot harder to raise a lamb than it is to raise a lion, Father. The lion soon learns to make his own way, taking what he needs, while a lamb needs constant protection and care. But sometimes there is a drought and the lions go hungry, while the shepherd is still there to feed and water the lambs. Father, protect my lambs. Feed them on Your love. Teach me how to shepherd them through the hard times and help them act in a way that is pleasing to You.

A CHILD IN THE CROWD

And he took a child,
and set him in the midst of them:
and when he had taken him in his arms,
he said unto them, Whosoever shall receive
one of such children in my name, receiveth me.

MARK 9:36–37

In biblical times, young children were not considered much use until they could contribute to the family's welfare. Yet You reached through the crowd of adults, including the disciples, and pulled a little child into Your arms as an example of faith. This must have surprised the child, who had undoubtedly been jostled and shoved away by the crowd. He may not have seemed important to the adults, but You knew the importance of childlike innocence and faith. Salvation lies along that path. I know my children have much to teach me, Lord. Help me be receptive of Your lessons, especially when You send them through a child.

GREATNESS REDEFINED

And whosoever shall receive me
receiveth him that sent me:
for he that is least among you all,
the same shall be great.

LUKE 9:48

You continued Your lesson by saying that anyone who welcomes You also welcomes Your Father, who sent You. Social status, education, riches—all the things that society values—are not as important to You as faith, which even the humblest child can possess. This is a difficult concept to teach children today, Lord. Society encourages the worship of sports figures and pop stars, the rich and the famous. I need to redefine "greatness" for my children and show them worthy examples of those who have received You. They need to know that there is a better, more glorious way to live—one so simple that even a young child can understand it.

JUDGMENT

*The wolf also shall dwell with the lamb,
and the leopard shall lie down with the kid;
and the calf and the young lion
and the fatling together;
and a little child shall lead them.*

ISAIAH 11:6

Children are easily frightened by the prospect of judgment. They know they have sinned, just as we, their parents, have, and feel anxiety about their accounting, even though they have accepted their salvation through You. You gave us this verse to reassure us. Who would be afraid to live when the hunters and the hunted live together in perfect peace? There will be no more wars, no more politics, no more fear, only Your righteous rule forever. "And a little child shall lead them." When my children ask about Your coming, remind me of this promise so they will not fear what should be a great day for us all.

THE PROMISE

For the promise is unto you,
and to your children, and to all that are afar off,
even as many as the Lord our God shall call.

ACTS 2:39

Peter was surrounded by people asking what they must do to receive the Holy Spirit. His answer was simple: "Repent, and be baptized. . .for the remission of sins" (Acts 2:38). This promise was given to all, from every nation, of every status, near or far, adults and children alike. You will do the calling; all we need to do is repent and be baptized. The process is simple so that even the simplest can understand. Help me explain this to my children, Lord. I yearn to know they belong to You, for as John said, "I have no greater joy than to hear that my children walk in truth" (3 John 4).

COVETOUSNESS

Let your conversation be without covetousness;
and be content with such things as ye have:
for he hath said,
I will never leave thee, nor forsake thee.

HEBREWS 13:5

It is so easy to fall into the trap of covetousness, Lord. Today everything is bigger, better, new and improved. About the only thing that doesn't get repackaged every year is Ivory soap, but that still gets me clean. I miss old-fashioned contentment, using time-proven products, and watching the sun set instead of the evening news. Still, I admit I am not totally content. There's just so much available, and some of it looks pretty good. On days when a commercial gets to me a little, remind me that I have everything I really need, Lord. Best of all, I have You, whose promises never change, and You will always supply my true needs.

A MERRY HEART

A merry heart doeth good like a medicine.

PROVERBS 17:22

I know a woman who overflows with a merry heart, Lord. She smiles continuously and laughs loudly, infecting everyone around her with the giggles. She makes everyone feel good about themselves, no matter what the situation, because her concern for others is genuine. She is a very sick woman but enjoys every moment of life, whether it is full of joy or pain, and shrugs off her illnesses. I frankly do not know how she does it, but I do believe her happy heart has lengthened her life. Lord, I wish I could live in continuous joy the way she does. I would like to be remembered for my laugh but am afraid not enough people have heard it. I would love to be content no matter what comes my way. Keep this woman healthy as well as happy. The world needs her.

AFFLICTION

All the days of the afflicted are evil:
but he that is of a merry heart
hath a continual feast.

PROVERBS 15:15

I have been afflicted in my lifetime, as have most women, but You helped me walk out of affliction and invited me to Your continual feast. Right now I am still at Your banquet, but I know affliction will come again. Right now I am content and comfortable, enjoying life to its fullest. I don't know if I will feel that way when trials come to me again, because I don't really have a merry heart. Like most people, I am happiest when things are going nicely, but when things go wrong, my heart is not so merry. Help me get over this nagging self-doubt, Father. Remind me that Your blessings are forever and I have nothing to fear. Give me a merry heart, I pray.

FULFILLED DREAMS

Let not thine heart envy sinners:
but be thou in the fear
of the LORD all the day long.
For surely there is an end;
and thine expectation shall not be cut off.

PROVERBS 23:17–18

Why should my heart envy sinners? The world may give them certain advantages, but I am already content with my life, so why would I follow them? I possess all I need, more than they will ever enjoy: happiness, joy, love, and forgiveness for my sins. Still, I can understand that there are many good Christians whose dreams are not coming true, Lord. They struggle to make ends meet and provide for their families, yet they walk through life with a happy heart. Thank You for Your attention to them, for Your provision, and for the promise that their dreams will eventually come true. I wish them the contentment I am now enjoying.

THE LESSON

*Now no chastening for the present
seemeth to be joyous, but grievous:
nevertheless afterward it yieldeth
the peaceable fruit of righteousness
unto them which are exercised thereby.*

HEBREWS 12:11

I'm fairly sure that You occasionally have to go to great lengths to get my attention, Father. I rarely think that my troubles may indeed be coming as Your means of correcting me when I fall into some great error, because I know You as a loving Father. But sometimes when problems pile up, I just have to stop and think: Did I do something that needs correcting? I take time to confess my faults and ask Your forgiveness, secure that You will forgive even my hidden sins. Even if my prayer does not solve all my problems, it does bring me back to You, and perhaps that was the lesson I needed to learn in the first place.

THE WILD CHILD

If ye endure chastening,
God dealeth with you as with sons;
for what son is he whom
the father chasteneth not?

HEBREWS 12:7

There is at least one in every neighborhood—the wild child who only thinks of herself and is never taught that certain behavior is inappropriate. I do my child a disservice if I let her think the world can be bent to her will. Soon enough the world will teach her the hard way, and I will be left to heal the wounds. Life does have rules, and I need to teach them to my children. Help me see when my children need gentle, loving correction, and show me the best approach to take. Let me be as kind and patient with my children as You are with me, but don't let me fall into the error of letting them run wild.

ACCEPTING CORRECTION

Behold, happy is the man whom God correcteth:
therefore despise not thou
the chastening of the Almighty:
For he maketh sore, and bindeth up:
he woundeth, and his hands make whole.

JOB 5:17–18

When You must correct me, Father, it does not immediately make me happy. It sometimes makes me struggle to get loose and go my own way, especially when I don't recognize that I am dealing with Your correction. It's easier to blame someone else. But eventually I see a pattern, or You open my eyes in other ways, and I stop running away from You, because I know that You not only correct but also heal. Your correction lasts only a moment; its blessings are eternal. When I realize You are so concerned for me and want to help me, I am filled with gratitude and willing to be led in the right direction.

WORLDLY CORRECTION

For our light affliction,
which is but for a moment,
worketh for us a far more exceeding
and eternal weight of glory.

2 CORINTHIANS 4:17

The world "corrects" me every day, Father, quite often unjustly and in no way to my benefit. At the time, the blows I suffer seem to be more than I can bear. But with Your help I do bear them, and when I bear them through faith, my actions are examples of Your power and love. The worst the world can do is kill me. I'm not exactly eager for that, Father, but when the time comes, I pray I will be able to bear death as well as I bore life, secure in Your love and looking to the salvation You have promised is mine. Until then I will do my best to be Your witness here on earth.

THE FEAST

*When the heart of the king was merry with wine,
he commanded. . .the seven chamberlains. . .
to bring Vashti the queen before the king
with the crown royal,
to shew the people and the princes her beauty.*

ESTHER 1:10–11

Ahasuerus had been entertaining for 187 days, the last seven of which had been a lavish feast. Almost everyone was intoxicated when the king sent his seven chamberlains to bring Queen Vashti before the princes and his party so they could admire her beauty. To everyone's shock, she refused to appear. Being paraded before a bunch of drunks for their amusement is not something any woman would enjoy. All women have their standards; none deserves to be treated like a piece of property. When someone asks me to lower my standards in order to make them feel like royalty, remind me of Vashti and her dignity, Lord.

CONTEMPT AND WRATH

*This deed of the queen shall
come abroad unto all women,
so that they shall despise
their husbands in their eyes,
when it shall be reported.*

ESTHER 1:17

The king's advisors saw danger in Queen Vashti's example. If she could get away with being disobedient to the king, her act would certainly affect every woman in the kingdom. It would take time for the gossip to spread—the kingdom was vast— but in time all wives would hear the story and look on their husbands with contempt and wrath. Or so the wise men said. We know, Father, that such broad conclusions are foolish. Most women have respect for their husbands, and the example of the queen would only be a problem for harsh, overbearing husbands. Let us live in love and peace, not fear losing some "authority" that must be earned, not demanded.

EXILE

Let there go a royal commandment from him. . .
that Vashti come no more before king Ahasuerus;
and let the king give her royal estate
unto another that is better than she.

ESTHER 1:19

Because Vashti refused to be paraded like a woman of bad reputation, she was shut off from the king, her royal estate as queen to be given to another, more respectful woman. Most women have had a similar experience in their lives, Lord. We disagree with someone more powerful than we are at work, and we lose our job. We refuse to abandon our principles, and the social invitations no longer include us. We disagree with our husbands, and they give us the cold shoulder for a day or two. Sometimes we have to take a stand, no matter what happens. When these times come, give us the character and courage of Vashti, Lord.

BEARING RULE

He sent letters into all the king's provinces,
into every province
according to the writing thereof. . .
that every man should bear rule
in his own house.

ESTHER 1:22

Ahasuerus's actions probably made things worse. I can just see the reaction of a couple reading this notice. A woman would laugh at a king whose pride was so hurt he published such a decree. A man would puff up in righteousness at first, until reality set in. After all, you can't legislate love and respect. It's foolish to even try. The lowest commoner in the kingdom could do better than the king when it came to domestic life. The next time someone demands my respect, remind me that I have the right to my own opinions and my own standards. When a husband rules his house, he does so with his wife's loving consent, not because of some law.

EVIDENCE

*Now faith is the substance of things hoped for,
the evidence of things not seen.*

HEBREWS 11:1

Lord, astronomers have recently discovered distant moons and planets they cannot see through even the strongest of telescopes. By observing the effects these bodies have on other bodies—changes in orbit, for example—they know these distant bodies simply *must* be there or their effects would not be there. This is "evidence of things not seen," perhaps even the "substance of things hoped for." I admit I do not totally understand how the astronomers do this, but I find it comforting. There is so much I do not understand about You. Still, I can see the effects of Your actions, the evidence that You are still active in my daily life and the lives of others. I do not need to physically see You to believe. Your evidence is everywhere.

NOT WAVERING

But let him ask in faith, nothing wavering.
For he that wavereth is like a wave of the sea
driven with the wind and tossed.

JAMES 1:6

I've been in rough seas, Lord. I know what it is like to be at the mercy of the waves, and I do not like it. If my whole life were similar to the experience of being driven by the wind, I would not only be miserable, I would never get anywhere. To me, faith is a very big ship with big motors and a captain who knows what he's doing. Faith keeps me on course. Sometimes I waver. I don't like the look of the waves ahead; I fear we may be going in the wrong direction. But I have a captain who never makes an error, and the ship He commands is big and strong enough for any wave.

GRACE

For by grace are ye saved through faith;
and that not of yourselves:
it is the gift of God.

EPHESIANS 2:8

Some days I get smug. My faith has brought me through a bad time. Isn't "my" faith wonderful? I must be very good to have this faith. Then I come back to earth. My being good has nothing to do with my having faith. I can't earn faith; I can only borrow it. My faith is on loan from You. It's mine to cultivate and grow and enjoy, but it's Your seed, not mine, and You give it to me out of love, not as a reward for anything I've done or not done in my life. I'm a sinner—I will always be a sinner—but You have saved me through Your gift of faith in Your Son, Jesus the Christ.

LIVING BY FAITH

*And the life which I now live in the flesh
I live by the faith of the Son of God,
who loved me, and gave himself for me.*

GALATIANS 2:20

Lord, You know I am a miserable sinner unworthy of Your blessings, let alone Your salvation. On my own, I am a hopeless case. I gleefully jump over one sin and land right in another. Yet You love me, You came to earth to save me, and You entreat Your Father to forgive my sins and accept me as a beloved child. While my faith is small and puny, Yours is perfect and mighty. The life I am living right now is not the result of my faith in You but of Your faith in me. Thank You for Your sacrifice that saves me and makes me whole. Without Your perfect faith, I would be doomed.

SIBLINGS

Thou shalt not hate thy brother in thine heart.

LEVITICUS 19:17

No one suffers my disrespect more often than a close family member, Lord. I know my sister and brother all too well. It's hard to feel close to the big sister who tormented me for years and would never let me borrow her good clothes. My little brother spied on all my dates and reported everything he saw to our parents. Even as adults, they are capable of hurting me more than anyone else because they know exactly what will get under my skin. I know this friction between us hurts our parents, Lord, and ask You to help us all get along a little better. Teach me to focus on the good times we had together, not the bad, to quietly absorb their little digs and concentrate on their good points for the sake of family peace.

BROTHERS

*Thou sittest and speakest against thy brother;
thou slanderest thine own mother's son.*

PSALM 50:20

My brother is such an easy target, Lord. I can embarrass him any time I choose. I know all his weaknesses, his little secrets, and what I don't know for sure I can make up and get away with. He may no longer hide under his bed and cry during thunderstorms, but he is still not the bravest in the family. I do slander him, making up childhood memories that never existed for a good laugh at his expense. No court would find me innocent. Forgive me for treating a family member I really do love this way. Show me his good points, for I have overlooked or forgotten many of them. For the sake of our parents, ourselves, and our children, help me bring peace, forgiveness, and love to our family.

SISTERS

*And why beholdest thou the mote
that is in thy brother's eye,
but considerest not the beam
that is in thine own eye?*

MATTHEW 7:3

My sister and I have been at odds since the day my parents brought her home. I didn't ask for a sister; I asked for a new doll. Instead, I got a noisy, smelly little creature who didn't even know how to talk. I got punished when she did wrong. When she hit me, I was not allowed to hit back. We're adults now, and I am still a little disappointed in her. At least now I realize that I have my own problems, and she did not cause them. When I need her, she is there for me. Help us overcome our childishness and face the truth that we do love each other. Neither of us is to blame for the other's childhood problems.

FAMILY JUSTICE

But why dost thou judge thy brother?
or why dost thou set at nought thy brother?
for we shall all stand before
the judgment seat of Christ.

ROMANS 14:10

I understand that it is not my job to judge my sister or brother, Lord. When we were young, that was the duty of our parents, and they did a fair job of it with only a few bad verdicts. My brother and sister through blood deserve the same patience and love as those in my Christian family. If I can forgive a nonrelative who hurts me, I can be even more forgiving within my family. If I can give charity to strangers, I need to be at least as generous to those related to me. Give me Your guidance, Lord. Reveal the needs of my brother and sister—whether they are physical, emotional, or spiritual—and incline my heart to them.

NEW-MOTHER FEARS

For God hath not given us the spirit of fear;
but of power, and of love,
and of a sound mind.

2 TIMOTHY 1:7

Before I had children, I was young and fearless. I had decades of life ahead of me and no one else to worry about. That all changed when my first child was born. I began to live a safer life. Now I really had things to worry about, responsibilities that at times seemed worthy of fear. As I became an experienced mother, my fears went away (although worry will always remain). I saw that I could keep my children reasonably safe, that living in fear was a terrible waste of time, and that You had given me the powers of love and a sound mind to guide me. Thank You for helping me overcome my new-mother fears, Lord. Life is too wonderful not to enjoy.

EXHAUSTION

When thou liest down, thou shalt not be afraid:
yea, thou shalt lie down,
and thy sleep shall be sweet.

PROVERBS 3:24

Sleep was indeed sweet when there was a new baby in the house, Lord. It was also nonexistent. My husband and I lived with fatigue for three months, stumbling through the days and longing for one good night's sleep. Not only did the baby's crying keep us awake, so did the hypervigilance of new parents that drove us to the baby's room when things were too quiet. Looking back at that time, I can see that it was Your way of helping us bond with our child—boot camp for parenthood. Thank You for teaching us that we could handle parenthood despite our fears and exhaustion. Thank You for that first full night of sleep, which was indeed sweet.

EXILE

For the eyes of the Lord are over the righteous,
and his ears are open unto their prayers:
but the face of the Lord is
against them that do evil.

1 PETER 3:12

I cannot imagine what it would feel like to know that You had turned Your face away from me, Lord. You would look after the righteous but never even see me. You would answer their prayers but choose not to even hear mine. I would not exist to You. What loneliness! What fear and desolation! Of course I am thankful for the love and care You show to me, but I take no pleasure from the suffering of those You have turned away from. If it is in Your will, rid them of their evil ways so they can be touched by Your love again, made whole, and brought back into fellowship with those who follow You.

THE EVIL ONE

*Neither death, nor life, nor angels,
nor principalities, nor powers,
nor things present, nor things to come,
nor height, nor depth, nor any other creature,
shall be able to separate us from the love of God,
which is in Christ Jesus our Lord.*

ROMANS 8:38–39

I know the evil one's main goal is to separate me from You, Father, by any means possible, and there are lots of possible means he can use. I have much to fear from him because I am weak, and my faith is imperfect. But this is one battle he can never win. He can never stop You from loving me. You sent Your Son to save me and make me whole, and the devil will not prevail. I am Your adopted child through Christ. I am Your beloved daughter. Thank You, Father.

THE VIRTUE OF FORGIVENESS

Judge not, and ye shall not be judged:
condemn not,
and ye shall not be condemned:
forgive, and ye shall be forgiven.

LUKE 6:37

Lord, it's so easy to pass judgment on others or condemn them. Sometimes it even makes me feel good. "No decent woman would dress like that," I say, but what I mean is, "I am a decent woman because I dress properly." When I do this, I am applying my personal standards, not Yours. I am elevating myself, not You. Anytime I become involved in judging or condemning, I face the danger of having my own standards being used against me. Forgiveness, however, is always a virtue. Keep me from the temptation of making rash judgments or condemning others, Lord. I have enough of my own sins to worry about and beg Your forgiveness for.

CLEANSING PRAYER

And when ye stand praying, forgive,
if ye have ought against any:
that your Father also which is in heaven
may forgive you your trespasses.

MARK 11:25

Lord, You make it quite clear that forgiveness is a vital preparation for worship. In fact, it should come before my other prayers, since the forgiveness of my sins depends on my forgiveness of others. If I go to services without forgiving, I set up a roadblock between myself and You, which is the last thing I want, since only You can forgive me. Forgiving those who have wronged me is not something I enjoy doing, but it is simply good hygiene, like washing my hands before eating. Remind me of this every time I go to worship, Lord. Give me the strength to forgive others so You will forgive me my own trespasses.

My Guide

For if ye forgive men their trespasses,
your heavenly Father will also forgive you.

Matthew 6:14

I need to be forgiven for my sins, Father; they are many, and they keep me from fellowship with You. But if I have to forgive those who have deeply hurt me, I find I have a real problem. I can say the words, "I forgive my sister for what she said," but in the back of my mind I hear, "No, I can't. Not really." I don't want to add lying to my sins, so what can I do? I need Your help, Father. By myself, I cannot truly forgive some wrongs, but Your strength is sufficient. Show me the way to true forgiveness, I pray. I want to do Your will despite my weakness. Be my guide along this difficult path that leads to my own sorely needed forgiveness.

SERIAL SINNING

And if he trespass against thee
seven times in a day,
and seven times in a day turn again to thee,
saying, I repent; thou shalt forgive him.

LUKE 17:4

Some people are just like little children who never seem able to avoid mischief, Lord. They trip their brother and apologize, then run off to sock their sister, all the time saying, "I'm sorry, Mommy. I'm sorry." I'm not much better, Lord. I shake off one sin, repent of it, then run right into another, all the time claiming, "I'm sorry. I'm really sorry." And I *am* sorry every time—just as my child is, just as my neighbor is. My only hope is in You, whose patience is perfect. If You can forgive me, surely I can forgive my child or my neighbor, no matter how many times forgiveness is required. Thank You, Lord.

PATIENCE

I am the vine, ye are the branches:
He that abideth in me, and I in him,
the same bringeth forth much fruit:
for without me ye can do nothing.

JOHN 15:5

Growing a fruit tree requires years of patience to allow the roots to reach down into the soil and establish themselves. Then the vine is strong, and the branches are ready to bear. I must allow myself time to take root in You, Lord, before I will see the fruit of Your love. The day I became a Christian, I thought everything would change immediately, but the world was still the same the next day, and so was I. I didn't know my roots were quietly growing and that it would take years before I became a mature, fruitful Christian. Thank You for the patience You invested in me, Lord.

A Nice, Sunny Spot

And he shall be like a tree
planted by the rivers of water,
that bringeth forth his fruit in his season;
his leaf also shall not wither;
and whatsoever he doeth shall prosper.

PSALM 1:3

If I were a fruit tree, I would want to be planted in a nice, sunny spot by a river. That would take care of my strongest needs—sunlight and water. Other trees planted in the shade or a dry field would have a harder time, and their fruits would not be as good as mine. Where we are planted makes a big difference. I am planted in You, Lord. I will take care to keep my roots strong in You. I will have patience, knowing my season is coming according to Your timetable and trusting that with Your help, every fruit I produce will be good.

BEARING FRUIT

Herein is my Father glorified,
that ye bear much fruit;
so shall ye be my disciples.

JOHN 15:8

When I was called to be Your disciple, Lord, my first thought was for my own salvation. A great weight had been taken off my shoulders; You promised me many things I wanted and needed. All I had to do was accept what You offered. I was pretty selfish about my salvation. I finally realized that my soul had another purpose: to glorify the Father who had accepted me because of Your sacrifice. Whatever fruit my life was to bear would be a song of praise. Keep me mindful of this responsibility throughout my life, Lord. All I am and do should point the way to others, that they also can enjoy the benefits of salvation and join their voices in praise of Your Father in heaven.

SINGING WITHOUT WORDS

Being filled with the fruits of righteousness,
which are by Jesus Christ,
unto the glory and praise of God.

PHILIPPIANS 1:11

As a child, I never raised my hand in school unless it was obvious no one else wanted to answer. Then I would raise my hand to make my teacher feel better. The idea of speaking in public makes me physically ill. Even now, I could no more witness than I can fly. But You showed me other ways to witness and give praise and glory to God. When I help a neighbor in trouble, I am Your witness. When I tell a child about You, I am bearing good fruit. The same is true when I smile at a waitress or thank my doctor for his good care. Thank You for teaching me this, Lord. You have shown me how to sing without words and serve without notice.

ETERNALLY USEFUL

*All scripture is given by inspiration of God,
and is profitable for doctrine,
for reproof, for correction,
for instruction in righteousness.*

2 TIMOTHY 3:16

Your Word was given to us thousands of years ago, to a different time and different people, yet it remains as useful to us as ever. When You gave the Word to its writers through inspiration, You gave us a book that would stand forever because it deals with the human heart, not a specific time and place. You meant the Word to be eternally useful to all nations, all languages, all civilizations. I admit there are some parts of the Bible that baffle me, Father. My understanding is weak. But when I am in need of guidance, the first place I turn to is the Bible. Any answer I need is in there if I search for it diligently.

FINDING THE SHORELINE

*Thy word is a lamp unto my feet,
and a light unto my path.*

PSALM 119:105

If there's one thing I need, it's trustworthy guidance, Lord. There is plenty of advice available to me in these modern times. The Internet is full of it—some good, some bad. If I prefer hard copy, thousands of books are published every year on religion and ethics. Even television offers all types of advice for all types of problems, if I take it to heart or not. If I took all the advice I hear seriously, I would be driven like a wave from one place to another without ever finding the shoreline. There is only one way to reach the path to the beach: trusting in Your Word. In darkness or light, on fair days or foul, I can trust the light of Your Word to bring me safely home.

BABY FOOD

*As newborn babes,
desire the sincere milk of the word,
that ye may grow thereby.*

1 PETER 2:2

When I was a baby, I tried to eat anything I could hold in my hand, whether it was good for me or not. When I became a Christian, I did the same thing. I was in church several days a week. I read theology books I could not understand. I spent hours discussing faith with other students. It nearly made me sick. I was trying to eat the meat of faith with baby teeth. Fortunately, a kind pastor handed me a Bible and said, "Read this until you grow up a little. You're just a baby Christian now." I needed milk, not meat, and Your Bible nourished me completely. Even now, when I can digest everything better, Your Word is still the best food for me.

GUIDANCE

But be ye doers of the word,
and not hearers only. . . .
Whoso looketh into the perfect law of liberty,
and continueth therein,
he being not a forgetful hearer,
but a doer of the work,
this man shall be blessed in his deed.

JAMES 1:22, 25

Guidance is only useful when we listen to it and take action based on it. It's a foolish traveler who asks for directions and drives off in the wrong direction. Why bother to ask if you don't listen? Or why listen if you have no intention of obeying? Your Word is my guidebook, Lord, and I thank You for it, but sometimes I forget to act on what You teach me. Why read about sisterhood and then go out and slander my sister? Why study forgiveness if I intend to hang on to my grudges? Show me my errors and teach me the proper way to take advice.

LABOR

*Man goeth forth unto his work
and to his labour until the evening.*

PSALM 104:23

Survival mandates that we work, Father, and our hopes of educating our children or putting something away for our later years mean that many women can no longer stay at home when their husbands leave for work. This leaves a lot of us feeling conflicted and guilty because our mothers were always home when school let out. Still, if I want to send my children to college, work must be part of my life. I need an attitude adjustment that can only come from You. Let me be a cheerful worker, I pray. Resolve my conflicted feelings. Take away the guilt that often comes with the need for child care. Give me Your peace and an understanding that all things work together for good when I follow Your will.

LABORERS WITH GOD

For we are labourers together with God:
ye are God's husbandry,
ye are God's building.

1 CORINTHIANS 3:9

The best thing about working is knowing I'm not working alone. I may plant the seeds, but You water them. I may do the weeding, but You send the sunshine. All I am and all I do is done with You, the One who created me and gifted me with whatever skills I have. You give my work—whatever type of work it may be—dignity and purpose. Your faith in me enables me to continue my duties on days when I would otherwise despair. At the end of the day, my feet may be burning, but I know I am walking in Your footsteps, and that gives me peace. I thank You for the work I have. May I do it in a way that is pleasing to You and reflects Your glory.

WORKING FOR GOD'S GLORY

Every man's work shall be made manifest. . .
the fire shall try every man's work
of what sort it is.

1 CORINTHIANS 3:13

In the end, Father, You will be the judge of my lifetime of work, and I know You don't care if I work behind a cash register or an oak desk with a five-line telephone. It's not what I do that matters, but how I do it. Am I a cheerful worker? Am I an honest worker? Am I a worker whose love for You is evident in what I say and how I treat my fellow workers? Do I care more for my brothers and sisters than for my next paycheck? I am Your ambassador, Lord, and every day I try to show Your love to those who do not know You. I pray that when the time comes, You will find me worthy.

VICTORY

Therefore, my beloved brethren,
be ye stedfast, unmoveable,
always abounding in the work of the Lord,
forasmuch as ye know that your labour
is not in vain in the Lord.

1 CORINTHIANS 15:58

In my daily work I rarely experience victory. I clean up one mess and move on to the next, knowing even greater messes are just around the corner. I never really seem to get anywhere, to win any battles, or to see anything truly completed. There are precious few victories in my work. But You encourage me to hang in there and keep on working for You, because You have already won the victory in the most important battle of all—the battle for my soul. My daily problems come and go; yet if I remain steadfast and dedicated, doing the work You have given me to do, I am confident that my reward awaits me. Thank You, Lord.

FAITHFULNESS

*The heart of her husband
doth safely trust in her. . . .
She will do him good and not evil
all the days of her life.*

PROVERBS 31:11–12

Father, through King Lemuel's mother, You gave him good advice on how to rule his kingdom and find a good wife. First and foremost, she said, a good wife can be trusted. Her husband never has to worry about her intentions or actions, because she will always be faithful and considerate. The care of her family is paramount to her; she helps provide for their needs through the work of her hands. Her priorities are always in order. Help me live in such a way that my family finds me trustworthy, Father. Give me faithfulness in all things large and small, so I may be an example to my children and a blessing to my husband.

STRENGTH AND INITIATIVE

She maketh fine linen, and selleth it;
and delivereth girdles unto the merchant.
She looketh well to the ways of her household,
and eateth not the bread of idleness.

PROVERBS 31:24, 27

The good wife's work of making fine linens is of such quality that she has money left over when her family's needs are met, so she sells her excess cloth. She does not squander her profits, however—she saves until she finds a good investment. This means even more hard work for her, but she is strong and willing to take on the responsibility, holding two full-time jobs while still caring for her family. While I cannot approach her perfection, with Your help I can learn to handle our family finances as carefully as she does, however. I pray You will show me how to be a strong, loving woman.

THE REWARDS
OF HARD WORK

Strength and honour are her clothing;
and she shall rejoice in time to come.
She openeth her mouth with wisdom;
and in her tongue is the law of kindness.

PROVERBS 31:25–26

The good wife brings honor to her husband and children. She seeks out and provides for the poor; everything she says is wise and kind. Right now, her work seems hard and never ending, but in time she will be able to rejoice, because she will have taught her children how to live, work, and prosper. The good deeds she has done will be known to everyone, and she will serve as the model of a virtuous woman. When I grow old, Lord, may I also see the fruits of my labor and rejoice, knowing that all my efforts were well worth the time and energy I put into them.

CALL HER BLESSED

*Her children arise up, and call her blessed;
her husband also, and he praiseth her.*

PROVERBS 31:28

What more could any wife and mother want? The good wife's children have seen her hard work throughout their childhood and know how blessed they are to have her as their mother. Through her example, she taught them how to live a good, productive life that is fruitful and secure. Because of her care, no one in her family ever wanted for anything. Her husband, who totally trusted her for all those years, knows his trust was well placed and does not hesitate to praise her publicly before the village elders, who have also seen her life and know her husband's joy is well founded. I wish I were half as competent as this woman, Lord, and I will follow her good example to help my family prosper as hers did.

BEYOND COMFORTING

And all his sons and all his daughters
rose up to comfort him;
but he refused to be comforted;
and he said, For I will go down
into the grave unto my son mourning.

GENESIS 37:35

Jacob refused to be comforted when he believed Joseph was dead. Nothing in the world had meaning for him—his many other children, his riches, even his God paled before his grief. He was beyond comforting. In time we all will descend into this dark hole in our lives that turns our world into ashes, a place all women know too well. When grief comes to me, Father, I know You will understand if I turn my face away from everyone for a time. I know this because You suffered the same way on the death of Your Son. In time I will return to life, but for awhile I will be beyond comforting.

SEASONS

To every thing there is a season,
and a time to every purpose under the heaven. . . .
A time to weep, and a time to laugh;
a time to mourn, and a time to dance.

ECCLESIASTES 3:1, 4

Grief is like a season in many ways. It goes through stages, each with its own special characteristics. Some of these characteristics are brutal, Lord; others are comforting. But like the seasons, grief eventually gives way to sorrow, to acceptance, to understanding, even to joy for the time we had with the one we lost. A wise woman is always prepared for grief, because it comes to all. A wise woman also knows that grief does pass with time. When my time comes to grieve, Lord, be with me. Hold me up with Your mighty arms until I can stand on my own once more. Hasten the passing of my season of grief.

COMFORT

Blessed are they that mourn:
for they shall be comforted.

MATTHEW 5:4

We may refuse to be comforted at first, but with time we see there is no shame in letting others weep with us. No one knows what to say to a mourner, but words are not really needed. When a friend of mine loses a loved one, give me guidance on how I can best help her. Perhaps I can watch the children to give her some private time. Maybe sending a son over to mow the lawn would help. Would she want my husband to help her find the documents she needs or give some financial advice? A few days' worth of frozen, home-cooked meals is always welcome. I don't want to intrude or seem overbearing, so give me tactfulness and the ability to see what is needed and how I can best be of help.

HEALING

Praise ye the LORD. . . .
He healeth the broken in heart,
and bindeth up their wounds.

PSALM 147:1, 3

In a few months Your healing will begin to be obvious, Lord. My friend will be finished with most of the necessary chores death entails. She will be back at work and beginning to appear at church and community events. Her children will be adjusting well. Although she seems to be returning to normal, I must remember that my friend is still very much in pain. This is a time when I must listen carefully, Lord. If she needs someone to discuss future plans with, make me available to her. If she needs expert help, let me help her find good advisors. Above all, give her Your guidance and support as she makes important decisions about the life she is rebuilding for herself.

PLANNING

A man's heart deviseth his way:
but the LORD directeth his steps.

PROVERBS 16:9

I have made lots of plans in my lifetime, Father, some of them just wishful thinking, some very concrete and detailed. They were all good mental discipline, but not that many worked out the way I thought they would. Some I was not at all suited for; others would take me two lifetimes to complete. Still, it's good to have some idea of where I want to go and what I will need along the way. Not all my plans are in Your will, though—even those that sound like good ideas to me. When they are not, You show me a better idea, and I thank You for Your guidance. Keep me on the right path when my own plans are flawed, because only You know where You need me to be today and tomorrow.

GETTING LOST

*I will instruct thee and teach thee
in the way which thou shalt go:
I will guide thee with mine eye.*

PSALM 32:8

I am easily lost, Lord. My sense of direction is terrible, and maps just confuse me. On days before important appointments, I go out and see if the roads I know take me where I want to go, which usually means I get lost two days in a row. I certainly need Your guidance on the road. Of course I need it in more important matters, too. Thank You for Your promise to guide me in all things great and small. Your eye is always on me, keeping me from error and ensuring that I can always find my way home to You, no matter how often I wander off the right road or face detours and dead ends.

HOLD MY HAND

I am continually with thee:
thou hast holden me by my right hand.
Thou shalt guide me with thy counsel,
and afterward receive me to glory.

PSALM 73:23–24

Often I am like a little child in a big toy store, running from aisle to aisle and asking for everything that looks good. Sometimes You grant me my wish; other times You say no. Like a loving parent, You hold me by the hand so I don't get lost in the store, just as my mother always did. Like my mother, You point out when my wishes are poorly made or too expensive for my soul. I admit that once in awhile I have a temper tantrum, disputing Your guidance and wanting my own way, but You have never been wrong. Thank You for Your love and patience, for I will always need Your guidance.

THE PATHWAY

*And thine ears shall hear
a word behind thee, saying,
This is the way, walk ye in it,
when ye turn to the right hand,
and when ye turn to the left.*

ISAIAH 30:21

If life is like a pathway in the woods, I'm always making problems for myself along the way. The woods are deep and dark, and I am easily distracted. I go off to the left to find a hidden spring that I can hear bubbling up, only to lose the path. I follow the tracks of a deer until sunset and barely find shelter before darkness falls. I make the same mistakes on the path of life, losing sight of the trail and calling out for You to find me before it's too late and I am lost forever. Thank You for finding me, Lord, for putting my feet back on the path and leading me home.

UNWORTHINESS

If we confess our sins,
he is faithful and just to forgive us our sins,
and to cleanse us from all unrighteousness.

1 JOHN 1:9

On my worst days I feel totally unworthy. I gather up my little pile of sins like dirty laundry and shake them toward the sky. "How can You possibly forgive this sin?" I ask, repeating the process until all my sins have been displayed. On my best days I calmly confess my sins (the exact same sins I had the day before), accept Your forgiveness, and go on with my life without guilt. I suspect that both reactions to guilt are acceptable, however. Confession is confession no matter how I phrase it. You have promised to cleanse me from all unrighteousness, to wipe away my guilt and make me whole if I confess my sins, and I thank You on both my good and bad days.

THE EMPTY WASTEBASKET

As far as the east is from the west,
so far hath he removed our transgressions from us.

PSALM 103:12

It's good to know You keep no "permanent file" with my name on it, Father. It would take up a lot of space. Like a good businessperson, You only handle a piece of paper once: read it, act on it, toss it. Or in more biblical terms, hear my confession, forgive me, then wipe away my sins forever. Toss them in a basket on the far side of the world and burn the contents of the basket every night. I'll surely be back tomorrow with another load. Thank You for dealing with my sins so thoroughly, Lord, for granting me a new start every day and proclaiming that while I am worth saving, my confessed sins are not.

MY SELF-CONDEMNING HEART

*For if our heart condemn us,
God is greater than our heart,
and knoweth all things.*

1 JOHN 3:20

Guilt? I know it well. It lives in my heart and tries to convince me that You could never love me as much as You love far better people. My heart tells me I barely have a passing grade and should forget the honor roll. No singing for me in heaven; I'll probably be polishing silver and gold all day. But You are greater than my heart, Father, and when my heart is wrong, it doesn't fool You. You know everything that was and everything that is yet to be. You forgive my sins and make me far better than my self-condemning heart thinks I am. Rid me of my useless guilt. I would be honored to polish Your silver for eternity.

A NEW DAY

Therefore if any man be in Christ,
he is a new creature:
old things are passed away;
behold, all things are become new.

2 CORINTHIANS 5:17

Every day I get to start over, fresh and clean, because I am a new person after I confess my sins and receive Your forgiveness. Yesterday I was selfish; today I can be selfless. Yesterday I was filled with deceit; today I can be honest. I may fall backward into my old sins from time to time, but tomorrow is always a new beginning, and I do learn, if slowly. I have a lifetime of new days to spend any way I choose, and I thank You for that, because I'm bound to get it wrong now and then. When I do, You wipe the slate clean as the dawn and encourage me to try again. Thank You for Your never-ending forgiveness.

THE MOST DANGEROUS ILLNESS

But he was wounded for our transgressions,
he was bruised for our iniquities:
the chastisement of our peace was upon him;
and with his stripes we are healed.

ISAIAH 53:5

Some of my illnesses I can heal on my own or with the help of my doctor. Some of them, time will heal (or not). These are physical illnesses, seldom serious but always frightening. You are concerned with these illnesses and give me aids such as prayer, but Your real concern is the health of my soul, which was perilous indeed until You sent Your Son to suffer in my place and save me from my sins. Once I was freed from my sins by His sacrifice of atonement, all things became possible for me through faith, including the healing of my body. Thank You, Father, for sending Your Son when I was so unworthy.

PRAYER WARRIORS

Confess your faults one to another,
and pray one for another, that ye may be healed.
The effectual fervent prayer of
a righteous man availeth much.

JAMES 5:16

There are prayer warriors all over the world, most of them women, who pray daily for the health of everyone suffering or in need, whether they know them personally or not. They do their work totally without fanfare, sometimes as a group, often individually. If I have confessed my sins and been forgiven, somewhere someone will be praying for me, even if in a general way. I won't even know I am in their prayers and may never suspect that my healing has come through them. Bless these prayerful, unselfish people, Lord. Reward them for their efforts on behalf of all believers who are ill, and assure them that their efforts are not in vain.

BELIEF

Believe ye that I am able to do this?
They said unto him, Yea, Lord.
Then touched he their eyes, saying,
According to your faith be it unto you.
And their eyes were opened.

MATTHEW 9:28–30

I may pray day and night for healing, but with-out believing in the One to whom I am praying, my words are in vain. "According to your faith be it unto you" is a great promise. It is also a condi-tion for healing. Sometimes I forget this, Father. I toss out prayer after prayer, just in case: in case You are listening; in case nothing else works; in case You can actually do this. On an ordinary day, I do believe You are able to heal me, but sickness frightens me, and I start qualifying every prayer. Forgive my wavering, I pray. Strengthen my faith and make me whole once more.

THE SACRIFICE

But that ye may know that the Son of man
hath power on earth to forgive sins. . .
Arise, take up thy bed, and go unto thine house.
And he arose, and departed to his house.

MATTHEW 9:6–7

There is absolutely no doubt that Your Son had total faith in You, Father. You gave Him the power to forgive sins and heal, and He did not hesitate to demonstrate Your glory through His healing. He must have known that His miracles would lead to suffering and death. Being truly human, He must have felt some fear because of what was to come, and yet He healed to show us that You had given Him the power to forgive sins, that all could be saved through faith, even though He knew that every healing brought Him closer to death. Thank You, Lord, for Your great sacrifice.

ANXIETY

Why art thou cast down, O my soul?
and why art thou disquieted within me?
hope thou in God:
for I shall yet praise him,
who is the health of my countenance,
and my God.

PSALM 42:11

Generalized anxiety, the doctors call it—that nagging feeling that something is wrong but cannot be pinned down. A lot of women know this feeling. It seems to be our job to worry about others and see dangers others never glimpse. Yet You did not create me to live in fear, but in hope. It is Your joy to watch over me. Who could do it better? You are with my husband on the long drive to work. You hold my child's hand at the crosswalk. I am not responsible for everyone and everything— You are, and I know You are trustworthy. Help me to hope in You and trust Your protection.

REAL DANGERS

*Wherefore gird up the loins
of your mind, be sober,
and hope to the end for the grace
that is to be brought unto you
at the revelation of Jesus Christ.*

1 PETER 1:13

Sometimes danger is too real. A child becomes dangerously ill, a relative has a stroke, or someone we love is in an accident. We all react differently to such disasters, but eventually we all fall apart. Even those who seem strong as a rock shake on the inside. Somehow we manage to cope, to hold ourselves together and do what needs to be done in spite of our fear and grief. We live in hope: first in hope of a cure, then, if that fails, in hope of salvation. When all hope seems to be lost, Lord, be with those who suffer. Help them to never abandon hope, for all things are possible with You.

DYING IN HOPE

The wicked is driven away in his wickedness:
but the righteous hath hope in his death.

PROVERBS 14:32

The life we have lived can be a great comfort to those we love when it comes time for us to die. They have enjoyed our love; they have witnessed our good deeds and seen the evidence of our faith. They are secure in the knowledge that we are with You even as they mourn. They do not fear for our soul, and that lifts a great weight from their minds. Even in death, we comfort them. Teach me to live this kind of life, Lord. Let me leave those I love in peace, not fear. As a daughter, wife, and mother, it has been my pleasure to ease the burdens of those I love, and I would like to do so one last time by living and dying in hope.

PRAYERS&PROMISES

COURAGE

Be of good courage,
and he shall strengthen your heart,
all ye that hope in the LORD.

PSALM 31:24

I am not naturally a woman of courage, Lord. Superhighways make me nervous, but they get me where I am going faster than back roads do. I fear going to the dentist, although she has never hurt me. I pick up a small grandchild being approached by a large dog, even if the dog's tail is wagging happily. "You worry too much," my children say, and they are right. None of this is Your fault, Lord. I don't even think it's mine. It's just the way I am. Give me the courage I need to control my fears, Lord. I know that You love me and watch over those I love far better than I can. Strengthen my heart.

A Seat at the Table

Use hospitality one to another without grudging.

1 Peter 4:9

Hospitality involves an effort, whether it's a dinner party for twelve or throwing another potato in the stew for a child who doesn't want to eat at home that night. Hospitality means greeting newcomers after church services, maybe giving them the name of a good baby-sitter or pizza place. It means going to my child's piano recital and applauding every child, not just my own. It is doing little kindnesses cheerfully. Lord, You welcomed me into Your family with love and acceptance. I was not worthy of Your hospitality, but You found me a seat at the table and fed me with Your Word. Help me be as kind to others as You have been to me—cheerfully welcoming everyone who wishes to dine with me tonight.

WHAT CAN I DO?

*If a brother or sister be naked,
and destitute of daily food,
And one of you say unto them,
Depart in peace, be ye warmed and filled;
notwithstanding ye give them not those things
which are needful to the body;
what doth it profit?*

JAMES 2:15–16

Kind words are good, but they need to be supported by kind deeds. None of my good wishes and concern will feed a hungry child or find a job for her father. Hospitality always involves *doing* something. It may be as simple as introducing a person to an agency that will help or to a used-car dealer they can trust. If I know a person's needs, I can find a way to help. Lord, I know that I cannot solve everyone's problems. Make me mindful of what I can do and willing to take the time involved to ease another's burden.

UNREWARDED KINDNESS

*Inasmuch as ye have done it unto
one of the least of these my brethren,
ye have done it unto me.*

MATTHEW 25:40

There's a popular saying today that no good deed goes unpunished. Sometimes it feels that way. But no one promised that hospitality and brotherly love would be easy. Certainly there is no guarantee it will be rewarded here on earth. I just have to continue to treat people with dignity and hope I don't get emotionally mugged in return. Yet You have promised that my good deeds will someday be rewarded, and I trust Your Word. When my cynical attitude keeps me from performing acts of hospitality, give me the faith and strength to do what needs to be done, not because I want a reward but because it is an honor to do Your work.

115

ENTERTAINING ANGELS

*Be not forgetful to entertain strangers:
for thereby some have entertained
angels unawares.*

HEBREWS 13:2

When my husband brings home a football buddy and introduces him as Joe or Pete before they take over the sofa and eat all the snack food within a two-block radius, do I ever think this stranger could be an angel? Do angels paint their faces blue on game day? Well, I don't know—and that's the point. This visitor could be just another couch potato. He could be the CEO of a huge corporation who enjoys slumming. Or, just maybe, he could be an angel. Lord, whether he's nobody special or one of Your army is not really my concern. He is a guest, and I owe him hospitality. Help me be gracious when it's time to go out into the cold to buy more chips and beef jerky.

THE LONELY SPARROW

*I watch, and am as a sparrow
alone upon the house top.*

PSALM 102:7

Some days I feel just like that lonely sparrow,
Lord. Everyone else is crowded around the bird
feeder, caring for their babies, or flitting to and fro
on urgent business, but I sit alone, just watching.
What am I looking for? Will I ever find a flock of
my own to join? Will anyone ever fly up and join
me on the housetop, easing this sense of separa-
tion I feel so acutely? Yet You tell me that not one
sparrow falls without Your noticing and that I am of
more value than many sparrows (Matthew 10:29,
31). You see me there alone on my rooftop, Lord.
You feel my loneliness, and suddenly I belong—
and I can sing a song of joy.

NEVER ALONE

*I am a companion of all them that fear thee,
and of them that keep thy precepts.*

PSALM 119:63

I know a church that refuses to give in to fear, Lord. Its doors are never locked, and sometimes I go in on my way home, sit alone in a pew, and enjoy the shadowed quiet. When I go to services there on Sunday, the church is full and no one needs to be lonely. The congregation welcomes me with brotherly love. But I relish my early evening visits with You, for although I may be alone in the sanctuary, I feel the presence of two thousand years of saints—brothers and sisters You love and still call by name. Because of You I am never lonely. My roots are deep; Your family of faith is always with me.

"HERE I AM"

Then shalt thou call, and the LORD shall answer;
thou shalt cry, and he shall say,
Here I am.

ISAIAH 58:9

Father, from my childhood You have never left me to struggle alone. All the years of my life You have been there to help me carry any burden I must bear, whether it is physical, emotional, or spiritual. I call out to You, and You answer, just as my mother always did. She knew my voice and could pick out my cry from a babble of voices; You know my heart. When I cry out to You, You are there, just behind my shoulder, ready to catch me if I fall, ready to support me if I stagger. When my strength fails, Yours is always sufficient. Thank You for Your constant love and care, for picking out my cry and never failing to rescue me.

ACCEPTING THE GIFT

And I will pray the Father,
and he shall give you another Comforter,
that he may abide with you for ever. . . .
I will not leave you comfortless:
I will come to you.

JOHN 14:16, 18

Lord, You know that sometimes I reject Your promises. When I am really lonely and depressed, nothing seems to make me feel better. I know You are with me; I know You care when no one else cares—but some days even that is not enough. The fault is in me, not in You. On days like that, remind me that although Your promises are free for the taking, I still need to accept them, to claim them, and then to live in faith that they are mine. No gift is truly ours until we open it and accept it in thankfulness and joy.

THE OFFER

God setteth the solitary in families.

PSALM 68:6

Father, those who are happily married cannot understand how others can be happily single, just as parents cannot understand how others exist happily without children. You have provided for those who do not want a solitary existence, who need companionship and love to soften the daily rough spots of life, offering us marriage and parenthood. Not everyone will accept this offer, but that is their decision, and You respect their freedom of choice. I should do the same, no matter how strongly I feel they are missing some wonderful blessings. Constantly pushing others to find the right person (forgetting how difficult that can be) only discourages everyone. Give me the strength to let my children make their own decisions—no matter how much I personally want an armful of grandchildren to brighten my old age.

MATCHMAKING

*House and riches are the inheritance of fathers:
and a prudent wife is from the LORD.*

PROVERBS 19:14

All parents hope their children will marry someone who will not waste the fruits of their work,
but now that arranged marriages are things of the
past, young men and women have to find their own
spouses. It's a little inconvenient, but I preferred to
find the right person without anyone butting in—
especially my parents. The good news is that sometimes You quietly help us out in our search, either
bringing the right person along out of the blue or
helping us see the desirability of someone we have
known for years. Those of us still looking welcome
Your help, Father. You know what I need, and I
trust Your provision, knowing You always act in my
best interests and want me to have a happy life.

FRUIT FOR THE TABLE

*Thy wife shall be as a fruitful vine
by the sides of thine house:
thy children like olive plants
round about thy table.*

PSALM 128:3

I know that a good wife makes for a good home, bringing uncounted blessings to her husband. The psalmist speaks of the wife as providing fruit for her family—olives and grapes for the picking—but of course he means much more. Fruit is a luxury more difficult to grow and scarcer than grain; it brings sweetness and happiness to what could otherwise be a boring meal. I want to be like a fruitful vine by the house, Lord. With Your help I can, whether the fruit I bring is children, a cheerful attitude, or money to help provide food for my family. Show me the best way to contribute to the happiness of my home and family.

SANCTIFICATION

For the unbelieving husband is
sanctified by the wife,
and the unbelieving wife is
sanctified by the husband.

1 CORINTHIANS 7:14

Father, I believe that it is best for believers to marry other believers. Their goals are the same, their priorities agree, and life generally has fewer conflicts. But love will have its own way, and sometimes believers love and marry nonbelievers. When this happens, I must assume You have a reason. Many unbelieving spouses have come to You through the good example of their loving partners—not through their preaching or nagging, but through the love they share and the kind of life that love makes possible. Let me not be quick to judge or oppose such a marriage out of hand. Let me give love time to do its work. I may never see the result I want, but I am sure it is safely in Your hands.

GREAT RICHES

There is that maketh himself rich,
yet hath nothing:
there is that maketh himself poor,
yet hath great riches.

PROVERBS 13:7

Lord, money is pretty tight around here. We have enough to get by, but nothing extra—no savings for emergencies or retirement. Still, we have managed to educate our children, and they are living good, useful lives. It involved a lot of sacrifice to get them to this point, but it was worth it all. I know others whose children went to the best schools without financial aid or loans and are now living at home and going nowhere in the expensive cars they received for graduation. I see the disappointment in their parents' eyes and thank You for helping us raise children who appreciate what they have and work hard to build their own lives, with or without financial riches.

RICHES HAVE WINGS

Labour not to be rich:
cease from thine own wisdom.
Wilt thou set thine eyes upon that which is not?
for riches certainly make themselves wings;
they fly away as an eagle toward heaven.

PROVERBS 23:4–5

Over the years I have learned much about riches —in principle. I have learned that every time I save up a little, the roof will begin to leak or the driveway will need repaving. As soon as I make vacation plans and pay the nonrefundable deposit, one of us will not be able to get that week off. I've gotten used to this, Lord; I know how to roll with the punches. There will be time to save more money, and we'll take other vacations. I am not seeking riches, anyway. Thank You for what I do have, which is happiness. Help me to be wise with what money I have and use it in a way that pleases You.

QUIETNESS OF SPIRIT

*Better is an handful with quietness,
than both the hands full with
travail and vexation of spirit.*

ECCLESIASTES 4:6

I confess that I am easily vexed, Lord, but it is just the grouchiness of old age, not true vexation of my spirit. I have been blessed with a good life. I learned to live the simple life as a child, when we didn't have much money but always had fun. I learned to be thankful when my children were born. I learned to give when others gave to me. I have also discovered that the world is full of very nice people doing their best under the circumstances. Oh, there are a few stinkers in the crowd, but overall I like people. Thank You for all You have given me, Lord, for all You have taught me, and for all the good times still to come.

MEETING TOGETHER

*The rich and poor meet together:
the LORD is the maker of them all.*

PROVERBS 22:2

I refuse to let envy cloud my life, Lord, but sometimes it's hard to feel that I have anything in common with the rich. After all, I could redo my kitchen on what they earn in less than a month. If I were to suddenly become rich, I wouldn't even know what to do with the money left over after my needs were filled. There's really a lot that the rich and poor could learn from each other if they took the time, and maybe they should, because we are all Your children. We have You as our common ancestor, the Creator who loves us all. When envy creeps into my heart, let me be happy for those You have blessed—in any way. There is more than enough of Your love to share.

ESTHER AND MORDECAI

And the king loved Esther above all the women. . .
and made her queen instead of Vashti.

ESTHER 2:17

Esther must have wondered why her cousin Mordecai, who had raised her after her parents' death, had brought her to this pagan king, but she knew You had a purpose and was obedient to the man who raised her. As You planned, the king fell in love with the young Jewish girl and made her his wife. You knew that her obedience and brave actions would save the lives of all the Jews in the kingdom, including herself and Mordecai, but she would not know that until later. I usually do not know why my life takes sudden turns for the good or the bad, Lord. All I can do is serve You faithfully—whether in a palace or an apartment—until Your plan for my life is revealed.

TAKING A CHANCE

*Whosoever. . .shall come unto the king
into the inner court, who is not called,
there is one law of his to put him to death,
except such to whom the king shall
hold out the golden sceptre.*

ESTHER 4:11

Haman had convinced the king that the Jews were a rebellious nation who should be destroyed. Hearing about the decision, Mordecai sent Esther a message: She must convince the king to overturn his decree, or they would all be killed. The king had not called for her, and going in unannounced could cost her her life. She fasted for three days, gathered up her courage, and went to the inner court. She had no other choice. Thousands of lives depended on her. When Your purpose is revealed to me, Father, I must accept my responsibility and do Your will, even if doing so may be dangerous.

JUSTICE

Let my life be given me at my petition,
and my people at my request:
For we are sold, I and my people,
to be destroyed, to be slain, and to perish.

ESTHER 7:3–4

The king was furious. Who dared do this with-out his consent? He had given Haman the power to kill Jews, but that was before the king knew Esther and Mordecai were Jewish. Mordecai had once saved the king's life; Esther was his queen. He had been tricked. Haman would die, and somehow the decree would be overruled. Father, it often seems that might makes right and I stand no chance, but Mordecai and Esther knew Your power can over-come whatever evil men might plan. When I am in despair, fill me with faith in Your justice. Give me the courage to speak up for Your people, even when I face personal danger by doing so.

VICTORY

Thus the Jews smote all their enemies.

ESTHER 9:5

The king could not take back Haman's order that the Jews be killed, but he could make it difficult to fulfill. He gave the Jews permission to defend themselves, killing anyone who attacked them and taking their property. "And all the rulers of the provinces, and the lieutenants, and the deputies, and officers of the king, helped the Jews" (Esther 9:3). The faithful actions of Esther and Mordecai not only saved themselves, but also their people. The Bible tells us that many of the people of the land became Jews as a result of the power given them by the king (Esther 8:17). Father, the next time I am faced with danger for Your sake, let me remember that You are faithful to reward Your people, no matter how much I may fear.

WITHOUT WAVERING

*Let us hold fast the profession of
our faith without wavering;
(for he is faithful that promised).*

HEBREWS 10:23

Lord, with Your blood You wiped away my sins, leaving me promises to enjoy in faith until You come back again to claim me as Your own. It takes patience to live in faith, and I confess that sometimes my patience runs thin. I wonder why You don't act in ways that I can see and understand. Why is there so much evil and suffering in this world that discourage both the faithful and the unfaithful? I don't understand. Help me realize that my understanding is not necessary for the completion of Your plan. You understand everything; all I need to do is have faith. In the meantime, keep me free from wavering, Lord. Your faithfulness is perfect, and Your will will be done.

An Instant World

*For ye have need of patience, that,
after ye have done the will of God,
ye might receive the promise.*

HEBREWS 10:36

This is an instant world, Lord. Patience is not much valued here. If I don't get what I think I need, I take charge myself and double my efforts, not even thinking about sitting back in patience and waiting for You to act. Like a little child, I run to and fro looking for something to amuse me, even when I know it's not amusement I need. Just like a child, I get myself in trouble when I run ahead of You. On days when I go off on my own, draw me close to You until I calm down and begin to think clearly. Everything is under control. All I need has been provided. All I need to contribute is faith and patience.

SUFFERING IN PATIENCE

For what glory is it, if,
when ye be buffeted for your faults,
ye shall take it patiently?
but if, when ye do well, and suffer for it,
ye take it patiently,
this is acceptable with God.

1 PETER 2:20

There are days, Lord, when some in my family see me all too clearly. I have a full set of faults, and they remind me of each and every one. I try to be patient, but I deserve what I get, so my patience is not much of a virtue. On the other hand, sometimes I actually do well and find myself being punished for that. As much as I want to, I seldom show patience then. I can see it would be a virtue, but I can't quite get there. Give me patience on both the good and bad days, Lord. My judgment is flawed, but Yours is perfect.

MOTHERHOOD

And let us not be weary in well doing:
for in due season we shall reap,
if we faint not.

GALATIANS 6:9

Mothers understand becoming weary in well doing and trying not to faint. As a young mother, I was often ready for a nap at 10:00 A.M. Nap time every four hours was as vital to me as it was to the health and well-being of my baby. Now my children are grown, and I am reaping the rewards of my patience—grandchildren and a quiet house. I thank You for all of it, Lord, the exhausting years and the years of peace and fulfillment. I learned patience and stamina over those years, characteristics vital to my faith today. Because of my training as a mother, I may become weary but I will not give up, for I know the harvest is well worth the effort.

MARTHA'S HOSPITALITY

He entered into a certain village:
and a certain woman named Martha
received him into her house.
And she had a sister called Mary,
which also sat at Jesus' feet,
and heard his word.

LUKE 10:38–39

How honored Martha must have felt when You accepted her offer of hospitality, Lord. At the same time, she must have been a little worried. Was there enough food available for You and the disciples? Was it cooked properly? Were there enough clean bowls? Would You like what she cooked? There is always the possibility of disaster when unexpected guests arrive. I can easily understand Martha's worries, Lord, but don't let my worries make me shy away from offering hospitality to anyone who comes in Your name. One way or the other, I will manage to get an acceptable dinner on the table.

MARTHA'S PLEA

But Martha was cumbered about much serving,
and came to him, and said,
Lord, dost thou not care that my sister
hath left me to serve alone?
bid her therefore that she help me.

LUKE 10:40

It was hot in the kitchen, with too much work to do and too little help. Martha saw Mary sitting calmly at Your feet when she should have been sweating over the fire, as she was, so she asked You to chase her sister back to her duties. I've felt the same way many times, Lord. All those perfectly healthy family members are out there being sociable when all I have to talk to is a pile of dirty dishes. Would it hurt them to help out? In times like these, keep me polite and gracious, not bitter. After all, the dishes can always wait until the party is over.

JESUS' COMPASSION

Jesus answered and said unto her,
Martha, Martha,
thou art careful and troubled about many things.

LUKE 10:41

You showed so much compassion when Martha asked You to send Mary back to her work, Lord. You understood that she was worried about the many details involved in entertaining. Your words demonstrated how much You cared for her and acknowledged that You knew how much she was caught up in providing You a good meal, not something just thrown together. That dinner was the way Martha chose to show her love for You. Sometimes a kind word of understanding is all I need when I feel overwhelmed, Lord. The circumstances may not change, but I feel better about my burdens when someone simply acknowledges them. Let me give the same compassion to those who work so hard for my benefit.

JESUS' ANSWER

But one thing is needful:
and Mary hath chosen that good part,
which shall not be taken away from her.

LUKE 10:42

You always manage to gently show us when our priorities are out of order, Lord. Martha was so wrapped up in her work that she had no time to listen to You, while Mary knew that being with You and learning what You had to teach her should be her highest priority. There would be many more dinners to prepare, but Your time on earth would soon be over. Hospitality means more than good food; it also involves spending time with those we invite into our houses. The next time I get so involved in the mechanics of hospitality that I never get to talk to my guests, realign my priorities and help me enjoy my own party.

THE PROMISE

*I will certainly return unto thee
according to the time of life;
and, lo, Sarah thy wife shall have a son. . . .
Now Abraham and Sarah were old
and well stricken in age;
and it ceased to be with Sarah
after the manner of women.*

GENESIS 18:10–11

Father, You often seem to choose the most un-
likely women to bear extraordinary men—the
barren, the virgin, the woman too old for child-
bearing. Doing the impossible suddenly becomes
quite possible for these women. Whatever their
physical condition, Your promise to them is always
fulfilled, and Your will has its way. Whenever I
feel that Your promises are impossible for me—
I am too old, or too poor, or too unfaithful—remind me of these extraordinary women of faith
who did Your will and saw Your promises for them
fulfilled despite the odds. Make their faith my example and deliver me from doubt.

SARAH LAUGHED

And the LORD said unto Abraham,
Wherefore did Sarah laugh, saying,
Shall I of a surety bear a child, which am old?
Is any thing too hard for the LORD?

GENESIS 18:13–14

Sarah was keeping out of the way in the tent, but she heard Your promise to Abraham clearly enough. Abraham was one hundred years old, she was ninety, but You had just promised they would have a son. These were normal people in nearly every way, and the physical, human impossibility of Your promise was just too much for them. They both laughed at the news (Genesis 17:17). When You take us by surprise and offer us a promise far beyond our ability to understand, our first reaction may be to shake our heads and laugh. We know nothing is impossible for You—it's ourselves we are doubting. We beg of You, have patience with us.

THE PROMISE FULFILLED

*And the LORD visited Sarah as he had said,
and the LORD did unto Sarah as he had spoken.
For Sarah conceived,
and bare Abraham a son in his old age,
at the set time of which God had spoken to him.*

GENESIS 21:1–2

You promised that Abraham would be the father of many nations and You would be their God forever. You would give them the land of Canaan as an everlasting possession and never leave them as long as they obeyed Your commands. But before Abraham could be the father of nations, he needed to father a son—not the son of a servant, but Sarah's son, whom You had chosen. And so it was. We cannot begin to understand how Your promises are fulfilled, Father, but we know nothing is impossible for You and all Your promises will come true. All we need is faith.

THE POWER OF FAITH

*Through faith also Sara herself
received strength to conceive seed,
and was delivered of a child
when she was past age,
because she judged him faithful
who had promised.*

HEBREWS 11:11

Sometimes I wonder what would have happened
if Sarah had not had the necessary faith. On their
own, she and Abraham could never have had a son.
This is a moot point, though: You knew Sarah *did*
have enough faith, or You would not have made
the promise. I often feel that I lack faith, Lord, that
You must be speaking promises meant for someone else—someone more faithful and deserving of
them. Show me the error of this lack of self-respect,
I pray. If You give me a promise, Lord, it is because
I *do* have the necessary faith, whether I know it or
not. All I need do is act on it.

IN THE TEMPLE OF MY HEART

I will abundantly bless her [Zion's] provision:
I will satisfy her poor with bread.

PSALM 132:15

God, You chose to make Your home in Zion for-ever, where David's descendants would rule under Your Law until Christ's coming. In return for Zion's faithfulness, You promised to amply provide for the city's citizens, even satisfying the poor with bread. No one would be left out in Your chosen home. Now the temple is gone, but You still live in our hearts, and the promise still holds. When I am hav-ing trouble with my finances, Father, remind me that You will always provide, one way or another, for those who love You. Give me confidence in Your promises so I may never worry about the welfare of my children, whom You love even more than I do and have promised to care for.

DEALING WONDROUSLY

*And ye shall eat in plenty, and be satisfied,
and praise the name of the LORD your God,
that hath dealt wondrously with you.*

JOEL 2:26

You promised to do great things for Israel, Father, even more than You did for them in the past, when You brought them out of Egypt. You would defend them from attack and restore the fruitfulness of the soil, enriching them and guaranteeing them good lives. "The floors shall be full of wheat, and the vats shall overflow with wine and oil" (Joel 2:24). Frightening events would soon take place, but whoever called on the name of the Lord would be delivered. "The LORD will be the hope of his people, and the strength of the children of Israel" (3:16). Through turmoil and fear, You always protect and save those who love You. You will provide; You will save.

GOD'S PROMISES ARE SURE

He hath given meat unto them that fear him:
he will ever be mindful of his covenant.

PSALM 111:5

Father, being human with human weaknesses, we may forget our promises to our children, but You never forget Your promises to us. You remain honorable and full of compassion, even when we are weak and easily frightened. Your commandments stand forever, as does the redemption of Your people through Jesus Christ. Out of Your great mercy, You will always provide for those who love You and follow Your ways. Remind me of this when I am in need of food or shelter, Lord. Sometimes my needs seem to be the most important things in my life, but I know this is only panic speaking. I need never panic again: Your promises are sure. Help my desperation of today give way to Your reassurance and love.

WORRY

*Therefore take no thought, saying,
What shall we eat? or, What shall we drink? or,
Wherewithal shall we be clothed? . . .
for your heavenly Father knoweth that
ye have need of all these things.*

MATTHEW 6:31–32

Worry is our most useless emotion. It is unproductive and dangerous. Sometimes it may prod me into taking action to save myself, but even then there is no guarantee that my actions will be effective, because I do not think rationally when I am consumed with worry. Most of the time, worry disables me, locks me in my room, separates me from those who would be willing to help. It convinces me that I am unworthy, or stupid, or unforgiven—all lies of the devil, not Your judgments. Being concerned about my future is one thing; letting worry cripple me is a lack of faith. You know what I need, Lord, and You will provide.

KEEPING THE TEMPLE

*Know ye not that your body is
the temple of the Holy Ghost which is in you,
which ye have of God,
and ye are not your own?*

1 CORINTHIANS 6:19

Self-control is not a widespread virtue today, Lord. Many pervert the concept, turning it into "It's my body, and I can do what I want," when its true meaning is more like "It's God's body, and I need to control myself." My body is Your temple, the home of the Holy Spirit who lives in me and guides me. Why would I ever want to defile this temple for some fleeting pleasure? Of course I am tempted—I am fully human—but this body was made by You to glorify You, not myself. Be with me when I am tempted, Lord. Show me the true joys of self-control, I pray.

THE MARRIAGE BED

Marriage is honourable in all,
and the bed undefiled:
but whoremongers and adulterers
God will judge.

HEBREWS 13:4

Within marriage, You deny us none of the body's pleasures, Lord. We are free to demonstrate our love of each other's bodies without sinning, with creativity, passion, and mutual consent. We may give in to pleasure without sin, knowing that You have provided these blessings out of Your great love for us and Your joy in seeing us happy. But these blessings are meant for marriage, and You will not tolerate our seeking them outside the marriage bed. In the end, those who lack self-control in these matters face Your displeasure and wrath. Thank You for Your gift of sexual pleasures, but teach us to use them wisely, according to Your wishes for us. Keep us faithful to our spouses and to Your laws of self-control.

THE LORD DELIVERS

*The Lord knoweth how to deliver
the godly out of temptations.*

2 PETER 2:9

Self-control is not an easy path to follow. Those of us who try to follow You know it is steep, the footing insecure. Often it seems that others are standing at the edge of the path and throwing rocks under my feet, just to watch me stumble. If I lose my footing and fall, they take great pleasure in mocking me. Without Your help, I would fail to reach my goal, but You have promised that You will be there for me when I call for help. I do not know how to deliver myself from temptation, but You know the way. You have been there. You suffered temptation and won all Your trials. When I stumble, Your arms catch me; if I fall, You bring me to my feet and guide me onward.

MY SECURITY

Blessed is the man that endureth temptation:
for when he is tried,
he shall receive the crown of life,
which the Lord hath promised
to them that love him.

JAMES 1:12

We are all tempted. I would be an unnatural woman if I were not tempted, some kind of alien living in a strange world where the laws of nature did not exist. But no, I am fully human, and I know temptation all too well, Lord. You promise that You will reward those who endure temptation and emerge victorious, and I want this victory. When I struggle in this battle, be with me, Lord. Show me the path to victory every day, because sometimes I find it hard to follow. You know every turn in the road, and I will follow You in security all the days of my life.

A WOMAN OF VALUE

The workman is worthy of his meat.

MATTHEW 10:10

Sometimes I hear of fantastically successful women and feel I am loafing through life, Lord. If I were to go to college, could I be like them, or is it too late? The work I do could be done by anyone. No one would miss me if I never showed up at work again. Then I realize that the high school girl I am teaching the ropes to would be lost without me. So would the unhappily married mother who needs my shoulder to cry on. I will never sit in a corner office of my own, but I am important here—I am worthy of my salary. Thank You for the work You have given me, Father, with its opportunities to be of service to others and to You. I am a woman of value, and my contribution is great.

ONE HAIR

But the very hairs of your head are all numbered.

MATTHEW 10:30

My husband loves this verse, Father. Sometimes I hear him muttering in the morning and know he is counting the hairs in the sink, mourning their loss. He is glad that You care for each and every hair remaining on his head, but he's not too pleased as his bald spot widens. I know this verse is an illustration of how important I am to You, Father. If You care about such a small thing as one hair, I can only imagine Your concern when I am sick or suffering a loss. Bad things will come my way in life, but I am secure in Your love that never fails. I am constantly blessed by Your care and concern. I am so important to You that even the hairs of my head are all numbered.

CHILDREN OF LIGHT

Ye are all the children of light,
and the children of the day:
we are not of the night, nor of darkness.

1 THESSALONIANS 5:5

A lthough the night has its beauty, daytime with its light makes it easier for me to watch for Your coming, Lord. Those of us who know You are children of light, capable of lighting the path to salvation for others because we have gone that way before. "But let us, who are of the day, be sober, putting on the breastplate of faith and love; and for an helmet, the hope of salvation" (1 Thessalonians 5:8). You have paid for my salvation through Your death on the cross; You made me a child of light that I might guide others to You. Although I was not worthy on my own, You have made me worthy, and I thank You.

SALVATION

But ye are washed, but ye are sanctified,
but ye are justified in the name of the Lord Jesus,
and by the Spirit of our God.

1 CORINTHIANS 6:11

On my own, I am totally unworthy of salvation, and nothing I do or say can change that fact, no matter how much I try. I was a sinner; I am a sinner; I will always be a sinner. Yet, despite my disobedience and stubbornness, You value me, Lord. You believe I am worth saving, and You will go to any length—even to death on a cross—to show me Your everlasting love. You wash away my sins. You make me holy. You stand before the throne of Your Father and claim me as Your own, exempt from sin and judgment. Because of Your sacrifice, I am made worthy. Thank You, my Savior.

MINISTERING TO THE LORD

*And the twelve were with him,
and certain women,
which had been healed of
evil spirits and infirmities,
Mary called Magdalene,
out of whom went seven devils,
and Joanna. . .and Susanna, and many others,
which ministered unto him of their substance.*

LUKE 8:1–3

The role of women in Your ministry is not clear, but we can catch glimpses of them now and then. As with many men You healed, women also left their homes to follow You, to minister to Your needs. They saw You were fed and clothed, with a place to rest at night, taking on those burdens to free You and the disciples to do Your work. Many women carry on this ministry today, quietly supporting Your work, seeing to the details of church life. Only You know who they are. Bless them and keep them; give them Your reward for faithful service.

THE ANOINTING

A woman in the city, which was a sinner. . .
brought an alabaster box of ointment. . .
and began to wash his feet with tears,
and did wipe them with the hairs of her head,
and kissed his feet,
and anointed them with the ointment.

LUKE 7:37–38

The Pharisee did not wash or anoint Your feet, Lord, but a sinful woman did that and more, washing Your feet in her tears, wiping them dry with her hair, and anointing them with precious ointment. Her faith was so obvious that You forgave her sins and sent her off in peace. I don't think I would have the courage to interrupt an important dinner and beg Your forgiveness in such a dramatic way, but I would like to honor You in my daily life. The Pharisees in my life may not approve of me, but it's Your forgiveness I seek, not theirs.

A MEMORIAL TO HER

Why trouble ye the woman?
for she hath wrought a good work upon me.
Verily I say unto you,
Wheresoever this gospel shall be
preached in the whole world,
there shall also this,
that this woman hath done,
be told for a memorial of her.

MATTHEW 26:10, 13

The disciples did not approve of this woman "wasting" precious ointment on Your head, Lord. The ointment could have been sold to help many others. Only You realized she was anointing You for Your approaching death on the cross. You were so touched by her love and faith that You gave her a place in Your gospel so the whole world would know her story. I will never have the opportunity she had to anoint You physically, but I do so every day in my heart and know You care for me as You did for her.

At the Cross

And many women were there beholding afar off,
which followed Jesus from Galilee,
ministering unto him:
Among which was Mary Magdalene,
and Mary the mother of James and Joses,
and the mother of Zebedee's children.

MATTHEW 27:55–56

Most of Your disciples had scattered and gone into hiding, fearing the Jews would kill them for following You. Yet many of the women stayed within sight of Your cross. No one was worried about them, anyway—they were only women, so unimportant to their world that most of their names are lost to us. They had served You in life; they would not desert You in death. I know You have given them their reward in heaven, where they certainly serve You now. Remember those who still serve You today, who ask no glory for doing Your work well and will never desert You.

LYING LIPS

He that hideth hatred with lying lips,
and he that uttereth a slander, is a fool.

PROVERBS 10:18

Truthfulness is a great virtue to possess, but it's hard to maintain. Sometimes it seems easier and less cruel to go with a little lie, although it's never a wise move and will eventually cause more trouble than it's worth. But pretending to care for someone we dislike is nothing compared to slandering that person. Slander is a bold-faced lie about another. It's nearly always impossible for the victim to disprove the lie, so the social damage can be permanent. Father, if I can't say anything nice about a person, at least keep me from slandering her. In the heat of anger, control my tongue, because what I say then can be as damaging to my soul as it is to my victim's reputation.

RECREATIONAL SLANDER

For I have heard the slander of many.

PSALM 31:13

We are surrounded by lies and slander. Politicians twist the facts to prove whatever they want to prove. Corporate leaders play with the numbers until they come out the "right" way. But it's not only the powerful who slander—I can get an earful of it at any beauty parlor or market. Some of this is recreational slander, passing on to others the little lies I have just heard. I tell myself that gossip is harmless, at least until I am its victim and experience its pain. Father, there is no way I can avoid hearing gossip and slander, but I don't have to delight in it, let alone spread it. When I hear something I know another would love to hear, make me stop and think before I speak. What is to be gained by spreading the news?

"ONE OF THE GIRLS"

Whoso privily slandereth his neighbour,
him will I cut off.

PSALM 101:5

Not only are we expected not to spread lies about others in public, You admonish us not to speak slander in private. Telling just one best friend a lie about another person is a sin. I know that my friend is incapable of not telling at least one other person, who will tell another, and so on. Father, I know there really is no such thing as private slander. The only way to treat it is to let it die with me. Help me not to react to it, let alone pass it along. In time, people will realize I am not playing the game and cease including me in their gossip. Until then, guard my tongue and keep me from temptation, no matter how much I want to be "one of the girls."

THE WOLF PACK

He that worketh deceit
shall not dwell within my house:
he that telleth lies shall not tarry in my sight.

PSALM 101:7

Of course women are not the only slanderers around. Men have their own system. It's a bit more subtle but just as dangerous to all concerned. Men often climb the job ladder over the backs of others who are victims of their outright lies and innuendos. Good ideas are stolen; bad ones are attributed to someone else. Sometimes several men mount an attack on many fronts at once, leaving their victim powerless, with no defenders, just like a lamb surrounded by wolves. Lord, keep my husband safe from these attacks. Even more importantly, keep him from participating in the hunt and innocent of the harm being inflicted on others. The gains realized from this type of activity are temporary, but Your Word is forever.

A GOOD THING

*Whoso findeth a wife findeth a good thing,
and obtaineth favour of the LORD.*

PROVERBS 18:22

Finding a spouse in biblical times must have been as difficult as it is today. We want someone to share the remainder of our lives with, the good times and the bad, but it's not easy to find "a good thing"; it is truly a blessing from the Lord. Today hardly any man will openly brag to his buddies about his wife's admirable qualities. It's not macho. Rather they talk about "the old ball and chain." Help me realize that everything my husband says about me, especially in public, does not always reflect his true feelings. When his words hurt me, show me how to explain this to him and let him know I value his respect and love. I am "a good thing" — I deserve to be treated with respect.

DUE BENEVOLENCE

Let the husband render unto the wife
due benevolence:
and likewise also the wife unto the husband.

1 CORINTHIANS 7:3

People change. At first, a new husband and wife are so wrapped up in each other, it's like eating sugar with a spoon. You want to brush your teeth, it's so sweet. Over the years, they grow used to each other and their lives become the culinary equivalent of chewing a lemon peel. They snap instead of discuss; they belittle instead of praise. It doesn't have to be that way. Common politeness is due each marriage partner. Father, when I hear myself belittle my husband or speak to him harshly, remind me that Your standard for marriage is common respect and affection. I have found this man with Your help, I love him, and it is my pleasure to make him as happy as possible.

UNCOMMON COURTESY

*Let every one of you in particular
so love his wife even as himself;
and the wife see that she reverence her husband.*

EPHESIANS 5:33

It is the husband's job to protect his wife as he would protect himself. His self-love should be no stronger than his love for his wife. Even today, many men still walk on the curbside of the sidewalk to protect their wives from water splashes or runaway horses (it's an old custom). They hold open heavy doors and investigate strange noises deep in the night. In return, we wives should value our husbands' consideration and protection, seeing them as the signs of love that they are. Lord, the next time I laugh at my husband's outdated chivalry, make me realize I am laughing at his expression of love and not giving him the respect he deserves.

Worth Losing For

Likewise, ye wives,
be in subjection to your own husbands;
that, if any obey not the word,
they also may without the word be won
by the conversation of the wives.

1 Peter 3:1

A man is a strange and wonderful creature. He needs to feel in charge, even when he knows he's not. He can't help it; that's the way the Lord made him, and if I need to lose a disagreement or two, I consider my marriage worth the loss. It's not vital to my self-image, and I usually win in the long run. Many men have come to You through the respect of their wives and the desire to claim the peace that they can see in their lives. Don't let me concern myself about the word *subjection*. I have better things to which I can dedicate my life.

VARIETIES OF STRENGTH

*In returning and rest shall ye be saved;
in quietness and in confidence
shall be your strength.*

ISAIAH 30:15

The strength of women is not the same as the strength of men. In times of danger, it is usually the men who arm themselves and rush out to defend their own through the use of force. Women make their own preparations for trouble, storing away food and water, seeing there is enough clothing for all, preparing the children for bad news. Men's strength is loud and brash; women's is quiet and confident in the Lord. Of course this is a generalization. Some women fight; some men stay at home as rocks of faithfulness. Lord, remind me that there are many legitimate ways to respond to danger. If I choose to fight, grant me Your protection. If I choose to serve in another way, in quietness and confidence in Your mercy, that too is strength.

OUR SOURCE OF STRENGTH

*The righteous also shall hold on his way,
and he that hath clean hands
shall be stronger and stronger.*

JOB 17:9

On my own, I am rarely as strong as I need to be, Lord. Sickness weakens me; cares and worry tire my mind and make me less productive than I want to be. Old age will eventually defeat my body. Even when I am physically fit, I know there is weakness in me. But You promise that I will be able to continue in Your way as long as I have faith, and I trust Your promises. Make me stronger every day, Lord, no matter how heavy my burdens may be. Show me all the good You have done for the faithful throughout history and give me some of Your strength when my own fails. Let my dependence on You turn weakness into strength.

POWERLESSNESS

He giveth power to the faint;
and to them that have no might
he increaseth strength.

ISAIAH 40:29

Sometimes the world defeats me, running right over me on its way to who knows where. Caring for my family wears me out. Struggling to survive financially is a nightmare, while saving for my old age is a pipe dream. If I ask for help from the government, I most likely do not qualify, even if I complete the reams of paperwork. My health insurance never covers my illnesses, and I can't afford it, so I count on You to keep me healthy. I have no power to change any of this, and sometimes it makes me angry, Lord. Please increase my inner strength. Remind me that although I seem powerless, Your power knows no limits and You will provide whatever strength I need to see me through my current crisis.

BOTH FULL AND HUNGRY

*I can do all things through Christ
which strengtheneth me.*

PHILIPPIANS 4:13

The troubles I am having are nothing compared to what Paul went through, yet You taught him great lessons. "I know both how to be abased, and I know how to abound: every where and in all things I am instructed both to be full and to be hungry, both to abound and to suffer need" (Philippians 4:12). The result of his education was, "I can do all things through Christ which strengtheneth me." Some of Your lessons are painful, Lord, but I struggle to absorb them, to learn from them, and to come through them a more complete person. The fact that I do abound sometimes is easier to take, but even that lesson has its costs. May I learn to appreciate all that life offers, knowing there is profit in both the easy and hard times.

WORRY

*For he hath not despised nor abhorred
the affliction of the afflicted;
neither hath he hid his face from him;
but when he cried unto him, he heard.*

PSALM 22:24

Father, my trials are not major, so far. I have a child I worry about sometimes and a husband with some health problems that can be dealt with. But I know that things can go wrong in an instant and sometimes find myself waiting for the second shoe to drop. It's important to me that You will be there when I need You. You will not think less of me because I need Your comfort or turn away and pretend You do not notice my suffering. When I cry to You, I know You hear, just as I can hear my child crying a block away. Thank You for Your promises and never-ending care.

IN THE MIDST OF TROUBLE

Though I walk in the midst of trouble,
thou wilt revive me:
thou shalt stretch forth thine hand
against the wrath of mine enemies,
and thy right hand shall save me.

PSALM 138:7

We all seem to be walking in the midst of trouble these days, Lord. Suddenly we have enemies we never knew were enemies, people who prefer deception and violence to diplomacy. We do not understand them, and they misunderstand us. We are a hurt nation—an angry nation struggling to maintain its values while still dealing firmly with those who hate us. Guide our nation's leaders during these difficult times, we pray. Keep our sons and daughters safe in Your arms. Bring peace and security for all back into this hurting world so we may learn the lessons of this conflict and live together in harmony.

MY DEFENSE

The LORD is my rock,
and my fortress, and my deliverer;
my God, my strength, in whom I will trust;
my buckler, and the horn of my salvation,
and my high tower.

PSALM 18:2

No matter what befalls me in my lifetime, my defenses remain strong in times of trouble. They are not the defenses of an armed force, as necessary as that may be from time to time; they are the safety of Your promises and the assurance of Your mighty protection. Times do get difficult in this world. Conflict is always with us in some part of the world, and conflict brings tension, but tension should never become fear or the inability to enjoy this wonderful world You have given us. I pray You will always be my strength, my rock, my salvation. Hear me when I call to You for help, for I know You love me.

OVERCOMING THE WORLD

These things I have spoken unto you,
that in me ye might have peace.
In the world ye shall have tribulation:
but be of good cheer;
I have overcome the world.

JOHN 16:33

Lord, You warned the disciples that the path lying before them was both steep and dangerous. During the course of bringing Your Word to the world, they would become the first martyrs of the Church, hounded and persecuted to death on all sides. Still, You urged them to be happy in this life. Although the world would treat them wickedly, You had overcome the world, and Your salvation was theirs forever. The power of the world is no match for You, and because of Your sacrifice, all it can do to us is kill the body and free the soul for eternal life with You.

GOD'S DIRECTION

Trust in the LORD with all thine heart;
and lean not unto thine own understanding.
In all thy ways acknowledge him,
and he shall direct thy paths.

PROVERBS 3:5–6

I never know what the day will bring, Lord. A perfectly ordinary day may end with glory or grief, or it may end like a perfectly ordinary day usually ends. I try to prepare myself for anything that comes my way, at least mentally, but the truth is, there are too many possibilities for me to even consider. All I can do is put my trust in You and live each day in the belief that You know how everything will work out—even if I don't. You will show me which way to turn. You will guide and protect me day after day. You have a plan, and although I don't know or understand it, I trust in You.

FEAR NOT

God is our refuge and strength,
a very present help in trouble.
Therefore will not we fear,
though the earth be removed,
and though the mountains be carried
into the midst of the sea.

PSALM 46:1–2

When troubles come, I never have to face them alone. Thank You, Lord, for always being with me as my refuge and strength. Friends can fail, families can split apart, and my whole world can be shaken to its foundation—leaving me dazed and disoriented—but You never change. Your truths are forever. You do not shrug off my concerns and move on—You are "a very present help in trouble," standing firmly at my side whatever happens, guiding my actions, and giving me the strength to carry on. When all else fails, when friends and family desert me, I put my trust in You and am never disappointed.

NO PRISONER OF FEAR

For the LORD God is a sun and shield:
the LORD will give grace and glory:
no good thing will he withhold
from them that walk uprightly.
O LORD of hosts,
blessed is the man that trusteth in thee.

PSALM 84:11–12

Once I put my trust in You, Father, I am free to live in peace, no longer a prisoner of fear. Your sun warms my heart, urging me to go forth in victory and bask in the blessings that fill my life. You withhold nothing good from me, Your beloved daughter. Where I once trusted in earthly powers—governments, money, even the love and protection of others—I was often disappointed, for they are only human and have their own concerns to put first over mine. But Your love and care never fail me, and I am truly blessed.

FINDING STRENGTH

They that trust in the LORD
shall be as mount Zion,
which cannot be removed,
but abideth for ever.

PSALM 125:1

My trust in You not only brings blessings and peace, it also changes me for the better. Once I was vulnerable to fear and worry. I tried to combat these weaknesses by taking charge of my own life and finding my way on my own. I was my own responsibility; I would take care of myself. I failed often, and in response to failing, I believed that I was not strong enough or smart enough. "There must be something wrong with me," I thought, and there was. I had put my faith in the wrong person. On my own, I am bound to fail. Now that I have put my trust in You, I cannot fail, for You are always the victor, and this knowledge makes me strong where once I was weak.

THE CHARACTERISTICS OF VIRTUE

To be discreet, chaste, keepers at home,
good, obedient to their own husbands,
that the word of God be not blasphemed.

TITUS 2:5

Much was asked of women in the early days of Christianity. Your followers were expected to behave according to the highest of standards, to serve as examples of faith, so both their husbands and You would not be ashamed by their actions. They were to lead other women to faith through their everyday lives. Some went beyond serving as examples, supporting and complementing the work of You and Your disciples. Lord, I want to help bring others to You, to be judged a virtuous woman for Your sake, not for any glory that might come to me. Use me as You see fit, because any work You give me is an honor.

A House of Prayer

*Mine house shall be called an house of prayer
for all people.*

Isaiah 56:7

Although this verse refers to Your temple, it also applies to our own houses, which should serve as houses of prayer for our family and friends. A few minutes after entering a house, the spirit of the house becomes obvious. Some are filled with strife and conflict. Others are peaceful but feel empty, totally secular. The Christian's house may be quiet or noisy, but the Holy Spirit's presence will be obvious. Lord, I want my house to be Your house. The dinner may burn, the children may be out of control, but in the midst of it all, our house can be a house of prayer, a place of comfort and peace, a refuge to those in need. Help me make our home a blessing for all who pass through its door.

CASTLE-KEEPING

A virtuous woman is a crown to her husband.

PROVERBS 12:4

They say every man's house is his castle, a stronghold, a place of refuge at the end of a bad day. It provides safety for a man's wife and children when he is away, so he can do his work without worrying about them. Above all, it is the one place on earth where he can do as he pleases, where he can rule as a monarch (a benevolent one, we trust). Or at least it should be that way. Wives can either help support this castle or undermine its foundations. A virtuous wife keeps the castle in good repair and through her actions provides a crown for her fortunate husband. Help me give my husband the aid and support he needs. His life is hard, and he deserves to live in an atmosphere of love and security.

WASTING TIME

Favour is deceitful, and beauty is vain:
but a woman that feareth the LORD,
she shall be praised.

PROVERBS 31:30

I know friends come and go, whether they are rich and powerful or just ordinary people. Currying favor with the "right people" is rarely worth the trouble. They have nothing I want and will soon move on to other friends, because I have nothing they want. Seeking personal beauty is likewise a waste of time. I may be able to hide the toll of time for a little while, but eventually the wrinkles will prevail. Help me invest my precious time in more worthy pursuits, Lord, ones that will provide lasting satisfaction. I'm not sure what You will ask of me, but I am willing to try anything You recommend and give any resulting praise to You, where it belongs.

JEALOUSY

And her adversary also provoked her sore,
for to make her fret,
because the LORD had shut up her womb.

1 SAMUEL 1:6

Hannah was barren, but her husband's second wife was not and took every opportunity to flaunt her fertility and torment Hannah. Part of the problem was that Elkanah loved Hannah more than he loved the wife who gave him children. The poor man was caught in the middle. Both women were jealous and bitter—one because she could not have children, the other because she was second in her husband's heart. Jealousy is such an easy trap to fall into, Lord. It poisons a household and distorts reality until imagined slights become sore wounds. Even when I am as provoked as Hannah or as bitter as Peninnah, keep me from jealousy. It serves no useful purpose and renders me unable to do Your will.

THE VOW

And she vowed a vow, and said,
O LORD of hosts, if thou wilt. . .
give unto thine handmaid a man child,
then I will give him unto the LORD
all the days of his life.

1 SAMUEL 1:11

Vows to You must be kept, Father. You not only remember Your promises to us, You never forget our promises to You. Hannah understood the consequences of her vow: Once he was weaned, Samuel would have to leave her and live at the temple. She would only see him at the yearly sacrifice, where she would give him a new coat for the year to come. Despite the heartache this vow would bring her, she still desired a child and made her vow. Help me treat my vows to You as seriously as Hannah did, Lord. If sacrifices are required of me, let me bear them in faith.

THE VOW STILL STANDS

She bare a son,
and called his name Samuel, saying,
Because I have asked him of the LORD.

1 SAMUEL 1:20

Neither Hannah nor Elkanah forgot their promise to You. When their baby was weaned, he would go to the yearly sacrifice with his parents, never to return to their home again. He was so young, but they trusted that Eli would take care of him. Hannah and Elkanah would only see their baby once a year when they came to the temple. Both parents must have dreaded that day, but You had blessed them with a son, a son they had dedicated to Your work, and they were prepared to see him go on to do Your will. When the time comes for me to release my children into Your care, give me the courage to do so as graciously as Hannah gave up Samuel.

THE SACRIFICE

For this child I prayed;
and the LORD hath given me my petition
which I asked of him:
Therefore also I have lent him to the LORD;
as long as he liveth he shall be lent to the LORD.

1 SAMUEL 1:27–28

Samuel was weaned. Hannah and Elkanah took their sacrifices to the temple, and Samuel was part of that sacrifice. They took him to the head priest and gave him up to God's work. Hannah was not as upset as we might imagine. "My heart rejoiceth in the LORD," she prayed. "Mine horn is exalted in the LORD" (1 Samuel 2:1). Hannah kept her vow joyously. An answered prayer is always cause for joy. The Lord had heard Hannah's prayers, and Hannah kept her vow, content to give her son into the care of Eli. May I fulfill my vows as happily as Hannah did, Lord.

DEBORAH

*I will surely go with thee:
notwithstanding the journey that thou takest
shall not be for thine honour;
for the LORD shall sell Sisera
into the hand of a woman.*

JUDGES 4:9

Barak would lead the Israelites against Sisera, the commander of the Canaanites, on one condition: if Deborah would go with him. Deborah agreed readily but warned Barak that this battle would not be won by him, but by a woman. To his credit, Barak did not protest Your will. There are several outstanding women in Your Word, Father, each obedient to Your commands, each a strong woman. I hope I will never be called to war—or my children —and that You will protect the women serving in our armed forces today. They have chosen a difficult life, these sisters of Jael, but You will make them as strong and brave as the men they serve with on the battlefield.

JAEL

Jael. . .took a nail of the tent,
and took an hammer in her hand,
and went softly unto him,
and smote the nail into his temples,
and fastened it into the ground:
for he was fast asleep and weary.
So he died.

JUDGES 4:21

This seems like a brutal way to win a war, but what other weapon did Jael have at hand in her tent? She used what she had. Sisera had erred in thinking Jael was a helpless female, paying dearly for his lack of judgment. You know that women are often underestimated, Lord. Sometimes we are called to use what we have on hand to protect ourselves and our family or do Your will in some other matter. We would prefer to live a life of peace, but when we must fight for those we love, You give us the strength to do the unthinkable.

SISERA'S MOTHER

The mother of Sisera looked out at a window,
and cried through the lattice,
why is his chariot so long in coming?
why tarry the wheels of his chariots?

JUDGES 5:28

Sisera's mother played the role that most women play in wartime: She stayed home and waited for her son's return. But it was taking too long, and she was worried. Of the three women in this story, hers is the hardest role. Deborah had Your active support and knew victory would be Yours. You helped Jael rise above her fear and kill the enemy. But that night Sisera's mother would mourn, and our hearts must go out to her, because we understand her pain too well. Comfort all the wives and mothers who sit and wait, Lord, no matter on what side their loved ones fight. Give them Your consolation and comfort when the terrible news arrives.

VICTORY

So let all thine enemies perish, O LORD:
but let them that love him be as the sun
when he goeth forth in his might.

JUDGES 5:31

In this particular battle, You were strongly on the side of those who love You, and You played an active role in the outcome. Your soldiers shone like the sun at its rising; they could not lose. Our battles today are often not as clear-cut. Both sides may claim Your support and guidance, going forth in confidence and faith into a battle where victory or defeat may be equally unclear. It is not always possible to be as strong and secure in faith as Deborah and Jael; sometimes we must weep with Sisera's mother. All we can do is defend ourselves when we must and pray for Your help, knowing You hear the cries of all women caught up in war.

THE MOTHER-IN-LAW

And Naomi said unto her two daughters in law,
Go, return each to her mother's house:
the LORD deal kindly with you,
as ye have dealt with the dead,
and with me.

RUTH 1:8

Disaster had stricken the family, killing Naomi's husband and her two sons, leaving Naomi and her two daughters-in-law to fend for themselves. Naomi would return to her own land, but she could not support her daughters-in-law, so she begged them to return to their parents, where You would provide them with new husbands. Naomi was destined for a hard, cruel life. She was too old to remarry and would live on the edge of society. She put on a brave face and sent them away for their own good. A widow's life is hard, Lord, but You always provide for the needs of Your followers, and You had a plan for Naomi and Ruth.

RUTH THE WIDOW

*Whither thou goest, I will go;
and where thou lodgest, I will lodge:
thy people shall be my people,
and thy God my God.*

RUTH 1:16

Orpah took Naomi's advice, returning to her parents, but Ruth refused. She would stay with Naomi and help her survive. She was young and strong. There was work she could do. She would even work at gleaning the fields after the harvest, if need be—even though it meant being chased away by the harvesters and treated as a thief by the owners of the fields. One way or another, they would not starve. Widows have to make difficult decisions like this every day, Lord. All alone, with no one but You to care for them, they work at jobs no one else wants, for pay that barely feeds them. Help meet their needs; give them the hope that comforted Ruth.

NAOMI'S DESPAIR

Call me not Naomi, call me Mara:
for the Almighty hath dealt very bitterly with me.
I went out full,
and the LORD hath brought me
home again empty.

RUTH 1:20–21

While Ruth had faith in the future, Naomi did not. Her childhood friends welcomed her back, but she rejected their kind words. She said You had dealt her a blow she could not bear; the loss of her husband and sons had made her bitter. She was too old to survive, even with Ruth's help. Sometimes I feel the same way, Lord. Even if I have food and shelter, the joy has gone out of my life and left me empty and angry. In times like these, I need Your reassurance that You will never give me a burden without helping me bear it. Be my strong shoulder, my hope of a better future.

BOAZ AND RUTH

It hath fully been shewed me,
all that thou hast done unto thy mother in law
since the death of thine husband.

RUTH 2:11

The story of Naomi and Ruth was becoming known in the area. Boaz, a relative of Naomi's husband, allowed Ruth to glean his fields, making sure the harvesters intentionally left enough grain behind to feed the two women he had come to admire. In time he came to love Ruth as a woman. They married, and she bore him a son who would be the grandfather of David and the ancestor of Jesus, Your Son. Lord, everything I do has the potential of being part of Your plan for the world. I don't know the effects of my life now; I sort of stumble around and hope for the best. But You do have a plan, and that plan is good.

BASIC TRAINING

*Train up a child in the way he should go:
and when he is old,
he will not depart from it.*

PROVERBS 22:6

I am no educator, Father, and my knowledge of theology is far from great, but I long to teach our children about You through my daily life and example. Long lectures and great wisdom are fortunately not necessary for this type of teaching. My children watch what I do and say and follow in my footsteps from a very young age. What they learn as children, they will remember all their lives. I ask Your wisdom and guidance, Father. Instruct me in the best ways to teach my children about Your great love and the proper response to it. I trust You will guide me so I may serve You all the days of my life.

THE PEACE OF GOD

And all thy children shall be taught of the LORD;
and great shall be the peace of thy children.

ISAIAH 54:13

A child who accepts You as her Savior possesses an inner peace that no army can ever guarantee, Lord. Turmoil is part of our life on earth, and children sometimes have much to worry about, much to fear from others. But a child who clings to You knows a special peace that overcomes all fears. The victory has already been won, and she has nothing to fear from the hands of her Savior. This knowledge is the greatest gift I can pass on to my children. I have the faith that overcomes, and I wish this blessing for them. Help me teach all our children about You, about Your great promises, and about the peace that I pray will be their inheritance.

WISE UNTO SALVATION

And that from a child
thou hast known the holy scriptures,
which are able to make thee wise unto salvation
through faith which is in Christ Jesus.

2 TIMOTHY 3:15

Father, everything a child needs to know about You is available to him through the Bible, with a little help from the adults in his life. Learning Scripture leads to wisdom, which in turn leads to faith in Jesus and salvation. What greater gift could a parent give a child than helping him learn and love Your Word? I am not a biblical scholar, Lord. There is a lot in the Bible that I do not understand right now but will come to understand sometime in the future. Even so, I love You and Your Word and pray You will help me instill that love in all my children, so we might spend eternity together with You.

TRUE RICHES

That the generation to come might know them,
even the children which should be born;
who should arise and declare them
to their children.

PSALM 78:6

I have an inheritance to pass on to my children, Lord—stories of Your power and deliverance, Your great works, and Your boundless love for all the generations before us and all those yet to come. I have little money or possessions for our children to inherit, but if I do my job well, they will be blessed with faith and empowered to pass that faith on to my grandchildren. What more could I possibly desire for them? Temporal riches are as nothing; they stay behind when we go to meet You. When times are hard and I become discouraged, be with me, Lord. Keep me a faithful teacher of the Way for the sake of my children and all those to come.

KNOWLEDGE AND UNDERSTANDING

For the LORD giveth wisdom:
out of his mouth cometh
knowledge and understanding.
He layeth up sound wisdom for the righteous.

PROVERBS 2:6–7

I know that wisdom is more than knowledge, Father. Knowledge is helpful in life, and I encourage my children to seek it because it is beneficial to know history, languages, science, and mathematics. But even the uneducated may have wisdom, which is understanding how to apply knowledge in our daily lives. The most learned of people can still embrace evil, but the wise know better. You promise to lay up sound wisdom for the righteous so they will understand how You want them to live and thereby bring glory to Your name. If I have to choose between giving my children knowledge or wisdom, I would choose to give them an understanding of the wisdom that comes from You.

LOOKING IN ALL
THE WRONG PLACES

If any of you lack wisdom,
let him ask of God,
that giveth to all men liberally,
and upbraideth not;
and it shall be given him.

JAMES 1:5

Embracing wisdom is not difficult for a child of God; finding it is harder. In our search for wisdom, we often chase after it in the wrong places. The evening news may give us the facts, but its interpretation of the facts is often flawed. Professors try to build wisdom through the teachings of knowledge, but a wise student carefully evaluates any conclusions a teacher draws from the facts. Only You are the perfect source of wisdom, Father. You give it to us liberally when we ask for it, never considering us stupid or leading us astray. You have given us Your Word as the best schoolbook of true wisdom.

SEEKING THE WISE

For God giveth to a man that is good
in his sight wisdom, and knowledge, and joy.

ECCLESIASTES 2:26

Wisdom and knowledge working together give me the best chance of happiness. I want my surgeon to know every detail of my operation—all the facts of the procedure. I also want him to know if the operation is wise. Would another treatment be better suited for me? Am I emotionally, physically, and spiritually fit for an operation, or will it bring me more problems than it will solve? In other words, I want a surgeon who is both technically and ethically sound. If I find one like that, I have the best chance of experiencing the joy of healing. No one is perfect, but when I am in need of professional services of any kind, guide my choices, Lord.

GLORY

For God, who commanded the light
to shine out of darkness,
hath shined in our hearts,
to give the light of the knowledge
of the glory of God in the face of Jesus Christ.

2 CORINTHIANS 4:6

We cannot bear to see Your glory directly, Father. It would blind us if we tried; we would have to turn our faces away, just as our eyes naturally close in the face of a strong light. But You knew we needed to see the little we can bear, so You sent Your Son to give us a taste of glory. Through His life and example, Jesus gave us knowledge of Your power, Your greatness, and Your love. You do not overwhelm our poor bodies in their weakness. Someday we will be strong enough to be in Your presence without turning away. Until then, thank You for the knowledge of Your Son.

SERVING AS AN EXAMPLE

*I will therefore that the younger women marry,
bear children, guide the house,
give none occasion to the adversary
to speak reproachfully.*

1 TIMOTHY 5:14

These days there are many other activities that could be added to the list above: work forty hours a week, lead a Girl Scout troop, manage a church fair, take the dog to the vet, and so on. Whatever I do as a wife—and how I do it—must be done in a way that brings honor and glory to You, Lord. Sometimes I have to swallow my anger and endure criticism, but even that must be done with a smile, for I am Your representative here on earth and should give no one the opportunity to reject You because of my actions. When I am within seconds of being a bad example, send me Your peace, I pray.

BEING A PEACEMAKER

*The contentions of a wife are
a continual dropping.*

PROVERBS 19:13

The main concerns of my life are my husband and children, plus others I value highly. I want to be a peacemaker at home, at work, and in the church, not an irritating dripping that never stops and puts everyone in a foul mood. Hounding my husband to mow the lawn according to my schedule may get the job done but ruin the weekend. Insisting that homework be done *right now* makes the kitchen table a prison to my children, not a happy gathering place for family get-togethers. I must remember that my priorities are not necessarily the priorities of those I love, so please give me the sense to step back and allow everyone a little leeway to lead their own lives. I want to be a blessing, not an irritating drip.

In the Limelight

*Even so must their wives be grave,
not slanderers, sober, faithful in all things.*

1 Timothy 3:11

Some days I think it would be nice to be a minister—until I come to my senses. I could not survive the limelight that comes with the job. And yet, almost every day someone looks at me and, on a bad day, might very well find reason to say, "If she's a good Christian, I don't want to be one." What I do reflects on my husband, my children, my church. There's no way to avoid this, and I'm not sure there should be. I'm human, I make mistakes, and I have to live with the consequences. When I am a poor example to everyone I meet, grant me forgiveness, Father. Grant those I offend the wisdom to understand that no one is free of sin but Your grace is sufficient.

PIETY

Now she that is a widow indeed,
and desolate, trusteth in God,
and continueth in supplications
and prayers night and day.

1 TIMOTHY 5:5

Being a woman suddenly alone in the world is terrifying, Lord. Choosing to live alone is one thing, but the suddenness of widowhood leaves little time for adjusting, especially if the mortgage payment is due. Still, singleness has its blessings. Suddenly there is time for piety—for reading, contemplation, and prayer. There is time to learn to trust in Your provision and that of others who care. It will probably be necessary to find a decent job and discover along the way that I can take care of myself. Be with all women living alone, Lord. Be their faithful companion and guide as they struggle to build a new life based on Your love and care. May their faithfulness encourage others facing life alone.

THE SELLER OF PURPLE

And a certain woman named Lydia,
a seller of purple. . .
which worshipped God, heard us:
whose heart the Lord opened,
that she attended unto the things
which were spoken of Paul.

ACTS 16:14

Lydia had never heard the story of Jesus, even though she worshiped You, Father. She was a businesswoman selling expensive purple cloth she made—a very busy woman. She may just have been curious at first, always interested in new developments, but You opened her heart, and she listened carefully to everything Paul said that day. I have to admit that sometimes I don't really listen, Lord. I have too much to think of and too little time to absorb every sermon the way I should. But You promise You will come into my heart and live there if I welcome You, just as You did for Lydia. Come into my heart, Lord Jesus.

LYDIA'S HOSPITALITY

And when she was baptized,
and her household, she besought us, saying,
If ye have judged me to be faithful to the Lord,
come into my house, and abide there.

ACTS 16:15

Lydia was a woman of action. Once she accepted You as her Lord, she told the story to her whole household—slaves, servants, and perhaps children (there is no mention of a husband)—and everyone living with her was baptized. Then she saw another need and invited Your disciples to live in her house while they were in the area. She was so sincere in her hospitality that the disciples found they could not refuse her wishes. First Lydia welcomed You into her heart, Lord; then she invited the disciples into her home. I pray I may be half as dedicated and loving as this newborn babe in Christ.

DORCAS'S WORKS

*This woman was full of good works
and almsdeeds which she did. . . .
She was sick, and died.*

ACTS 9:36–37

Dorcas, a seamstress of talent, was also a busy woman who found time for Your work. When people came to her for help, she never turned them away; she was loved by all the widows in town. After she took ill and died, her many friends begged Peter to come to her house, at least to pray for her and comfort the mourners. He found her laid out in her room with a crowd of weeping friends at her side. I know that death comes to us all, Lord, but sometimes I feel I cannot give up a loved one, especially a person of good works. In a time such as this, send me Your comfort and peace, I pray.

DORCAS RAISED

Peter put them all forth,
and kneeled down, and prayed;
and turning him to the body said,
Tabitha, arise. And she opened her eyes:
and when she saw Peter, she sat up.

ACTS 9:40

The story of Peter bringing Dorcas back to life spread far and wide, with great consequences. Many hearing the news came to believe in You because of what You did for this good woman. They did not expect to be raised immediately when their own time came, but they had heard of Your power and glory among those they knew and welcomed You into their lives. Dorcas was a blessing during her lifetime and continued to be one even after her apparent death, through Your power. May I work to be such a blessing to those around me in my daily life.

SCRIPTURE INDEX

OLD TESTAMENT

NEW TESTAMENT

Notes

_____

_____

_____

_____

_____

_____

_____

_____

_____

_____

_____

_____

Notes

Notes

Notes

_____

_____

_____

_____

_____

_____

_____

_____

_____

_____

_____

_____

Notes

Inspirational Library

Beautiful purse/pocket-size editions of Christian classics bound in flexible leatherette. These books make thoughtful gifts for everyone on your list, including yourself!